At The Right Time

At The Right Time

A True Story Of How Two Broken Souls Were Saved By Grace, Love, and Redemption

NIKKI SCOTT

XULON PRESS

Xulon Press
2301 Lucien Way #415
Maitland, FL 32751
407.339.4217
www.xulonpress.com

Paperback ISBN-13: 978-1-66287-867-1
Ebook ISBN-13: 978-1-66287-868-8

TABLE OF CONTENTS

Journey Toward:

Hope Interactive Section

PREFACE

AS YOU TRAVEL through this journey here on earth, trials and tribulations will happen. At times, life can be dark. You feel as if there is no hope of love or redemption in this world. I have written this book of our lives so others can know love, healing, redemption, and pure joy can be achieved in this lifetime. I also wrote it to possibly help others heal from their past.

Forgiveness and love are out there, you must be open to it and ready to work hard every day for it. This is our life story. Two extremely broken souls who found love, comfort, passion, purpose, and fulfillment in each other.

Some names and places have been changed to protect those involved. The information and experiences are from my and Nikki's point of view. Some information has been given by third parties and their memories of what happened. Other people shared their knowledge of these times to help with facts and truth. Some refused to share their side of the story or "their" truth as they remember it.

Even though Nikki and I didn't always have the perfect or ideal life, once our lives crossed paths, we created the life we wanted together. We were determined to break the generational curses and create a life we would be proud of. This is our life, and I am proud of the man and woman we have become despite who we were trained to be and what our lives looked like they would become.

– Robert "Anthony" & Nikki Scott

P.S. At the end of this book, there are chapter reflections for individual or group discussion, study, and action. I encourage you to use them to apply the principles and life lessons in this book for yourself.

Nikki has also created a YouTube channel that will have personal home videos uploaded to so you can live in that moment with us. Look for the video with a title the goes with what you are reading.

Follow along at Youtube.com/@Therighttimebook

Robert's Story Begins:

"The past does not equal the future unless you live there."
– Tony Robbins[1]

[1] Pinterest.com

Chapter 1

THE MONSTER

SOMEWHERE IN TEXAS, there was a family living the life they were trained to live. They were living the lifecycle they knew they got sucked into, believing there could only be that life and it was all there ever would be. This couple fought and had their problems. They were people who let their past affect their future and now the future of their kids, as well.

My name is Robby. My life began in 1975 in a "normal" dysfunctional family in America. Mom and Dad would fight, and then makeup. They'd smile and act like everything was okay to the world, yet they were miserable inside the four walls they lived in.

Mom would cover the bruises on herself and me, then tell me to keep my mouth shut. Things went on this way until I was three years old and until the day my father got other women pregnant. I guess the beatings, fighting, and cheating were finally enough. Mom decided to leave that day. She just walked out and left me behind with this monster.

“THAT WAS THE FIRST DAY OF MY LIFE *WHICH* BECAME MY WORST NIGHTMARE.”

Even though I was just three years old, I knew the look in my father's eyes meant death for me. He wanted to get revenge on my mother for leaving him. I knew he had no intention of loving me or taking care of me.

My dad started off by beating me as he had before my mother left. Punches here, kicks there, and slaps for no reason at all. I wish things would have stayed that way. I wish I could say that was the worst of it, but over a short period of time, he got more and more violent.

Once the normal beating wasn't satisfying his rage anymore, he started to starve me. I would go days without food. He would lock me in a closet for weeks at a time. If I wanted to eat, he would throw soap at me, telling me to "eat up," laughing all the while.

I wasn't allowed to sleep in a bed or live in "his" space, so I had a corner down in the basement that was "my" spot to live in. He would come down, torture me, and laugh as he walked up the stairs while I struggled to take my next breath.

Dying became a wish for me. Torture and pain are what I craved because it was all I knew. At one point, I started pulling out my own teeth to torture myself when he wasn't around.

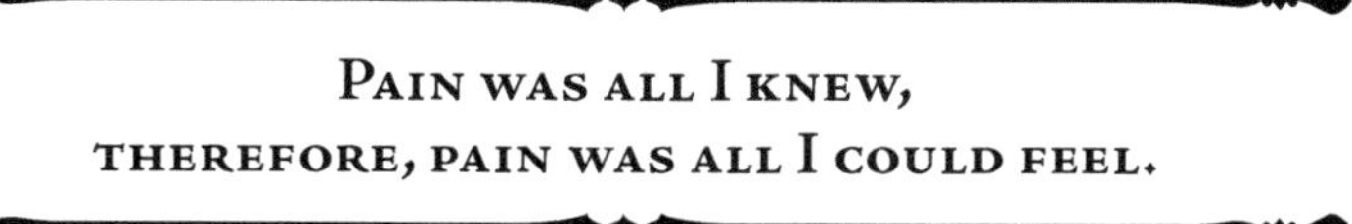

**PAIN WAS ALL I KNEW,
THEREFORE, PAIN WAS ALL I COULD FEEL.**

Then one day, Dad came home, and he said he had dinner for me. I was so excited to have a meal! Little did I know that soup would be the beginning of a new torture. Dad strapped me with an electric device of some kind.

Then, he handed me a spoon. He said if I could get the spoon to my mouth, I could have the soup. He sat across from me at the table and watched as I started to eat.

Scared and starving, I raised the spoon to my mouth. The hunger was overwhelming. Just as I got the spoon close enough to taste, I felt the shocks run through my body. This monster just electrocuted me! What kind of monster does that to their own child? I was so hungry I kept trying to defeat him just to get a bite of soup. I had a taste from time to time, but his laughter across the table was the start of stirring a monster inside me.

He would say, "Okay, I'm done you can eat."

Then, he shocked me again as I tried to eat. His laughter at every shock, each beating, and each torture would be the worst memories I would carry with me.

It was almost eight months of pure hell living with this monster alone. I prayed to God this monster would kill me just to let this nightmare end. I had a small glimpse of hope one day as I remember hearing a woman's voice upstairs.

Though I don't dare call out, I prayed this was the answer I had been praying for. Dad would move on, find another woman, and this way we could start over! Maybe, she would help him get over his anger. Maybe, someone would see me and get me help. Just maybe, it wasn't going to be this way forever. This woman started to come over more and more often, so the beatings started to lessen. Once she left, I knew what would happen, so I prayed she would stay forever.

As she come over more and more, Dad finally introduced me to her. She was horrified at the sight of me. Dad told her I had an illness that kept me from gaining weight. He told her since I was so ill all the time, I couldn't be around other people often. I don't know if she fell for it, but she continued to stick around.

Things got serious with them quickly. They married after just a short time. This lady decided I would be better off living with my mother. So, she put me in the car, and off we went. After a year of living in fear, torture, and hunger, it was coming to an end. I wasn't sure what to expect.

What would my future be?
Did I need to fear what was to come?
Would it be better?
It had to be better, right?

The Mother

Mom opened the door to see her four-year-old child, beaten, broken, teeth ripped out, soul shattered, and weighing only twenty-four pounds! As we walked into the house, my grandmother came to see who my mother was talking to. She was in complete shock as she looked at me. So many questions filled their minds as fear filled their eyes.

How could this be?
What happened?
Did my father do this?

My older brother, who was adopted by my grandmother, was forced into his room as if I was a threat to him. My mother and grandmother didn't know what to do or how to move forward.

My mom was living with my grandmother now. Grandmother started to fix me something to eat as they decide what to do with me. I ate everything I could and tried to put some food away in fear of being starved again. They knew I was in really bad shape, but they had no idea what I had been through. In their wildest dreams, they couldn't imagine what I had been through. I feared to even tell them what had happened. So, I decided I wouldn't say much.

I didn't need or want their pity.
I needed their love, patience, and understanding.

They took me to the hospital to have me evaluated. I stayed there for a while as they regulated my vitals and hydration. Many came in with questions about what happened to me. I tried to tell them, but it seemed as if no one believed what I was telling them, or they couldn't fathom what I was saying could be true. I was evaluated, treated, and later released from the hospital back into my mother's care.

Mother couldn't stand the sight of me. The pain, shame, and guilt within her were unbearable. Every time she looked at me, it made her sick and disgusted. I reminded her of the monster she wanted so badly to forget.

I didn't know what to expect living with my mother and grandmother. My brother looked healthy. He seemed happy even though we weren't allowed to play together.

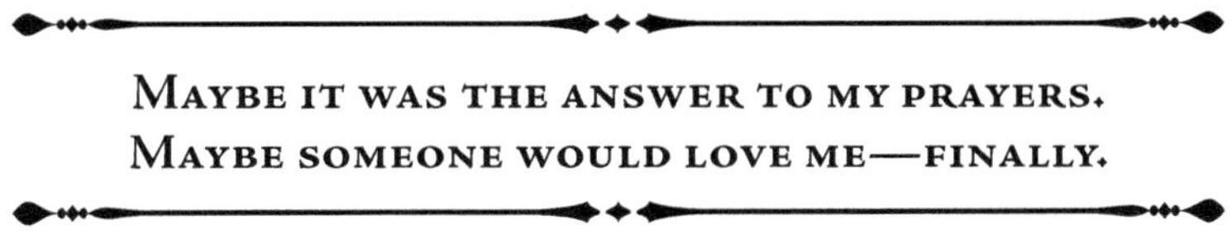

Sadly, just a short time after I arrived on mom's doorstep, she took me for a drive. She told me she was sorry for leaving me with that monster and she wished things could be different. She wanted better for me. Mom drove up to a very large building in the middle of some farmland. We walked up and knocked on the door. We went in and I sat on a bench while mom went inside the office to talk to some people for a while. When she came out, she had been crying and I didn't understand why.

I stood up as if I was going to leave with her. She gave me a hug, said something I couldn't understand, then she turned to the door, waved goodbye, and left me standing there. Alone, again. Terrified.

Turns out this building was a home for boys. They didn't start accepting boys until they were five years old. Mom must have begged and pleaded while she was in the room. They reluctantly agreed to allow me in at just four years old. They must have taken one look at me and felt sorry for me, just like my dad's new wife, my grandmother, and the doctors.

I already felt dead inside. Now, I was also terrified of what was to come, yet I was hopeful somehow. Pain was all I knew. Pain was all I could understand, but I hoped this was the new beginning I'd prayed for since being with my mother didn't work out.

Would there finally be food, friends, and love?

Hope got me through those first couple of hours.

Hope deferred makes the heart sick,
But when desire is fulfilled, it is a tree of life.
(Proverbs 13:12 AMP)

"Dissociation is an emotional protection strategy that totally and completely removes painful realities from the mind and body of the survivor."

- Kathy Broady[2]

[2] Goodreads.com

Chapter 2

The Boys' Home

I WASN'T HERE long before I knew my personal hell was going to continue. They took me to my first class, introduced me to the class, and my first teacher. The teacher looked over at my fragile, broken soul. She must have seen me as her new targeted toy. They continued their lesson as I took my seat. Waiting for time to pass until I could eat.

Lunch time finally came. I was able to eat a few bites before getting full. So, I filled my pockets with food, just in case I would need it for later. The recess bell rang, I wanted to go outside to see what everyone was doing. I was very skeptical of people and very shy. I had become a little socially awkward since I haven't been around people. I lacked "people" skills.

I stood off to the side, hoping to fade into the background and be left alone so I could watch. However, my teacher wanted to welcome me to the Boys' Farm with a welcome I would never forget. She took a trash can and covered me with it. Inside it was cold, damp, and dark. I was scared. Thoughts ran through my mind of what did I do to deserve this from a stranger. My dad, my mother, and now even strangers hated me.

As the fear started to take over, my teacher told the class to grab some sticks. They then started making "music" with the trash can. They started banging the trash can with sticks. The laughter from her and rest of my classmates took me back to my dad sitting across the table laughing at me again. It caused me to let go of the little bit of hope I was holding on to and go completely cold and numb inside. When they decided I'd had enough, they removed the trash can and just stared with disgust and laughter.

As I scanned the area, I saw a woman off to the side lines, just standing there. She didn't stop them. She didn't say anything to my teacher. She just stood there. In my book, she would become worse than my teacher could ever be. Knowing this was happening and not saying anything! Recess was over and now I knew my new "home" was going to be just as horrible as the last one. Returning to class, I was terrified of what was to come.

Torture, pain, and fear were what I knew and how I learned to survive. Even though more torture wasn't what I hoped for, knowing what it was like helped me to "survive" what was to come.

As night fell, I was tired and emotionally drained from the day's emotional roller coaster. I dragged myself into the showers. Then, it was supposed to be off to bed. Just like my teacher now had a new toy to mess with, so did the bigger kids, the other teachers, and sadly the counselors. My first night was spent with someone stuffing his junk in my mouth, then beating me until I swore not to say anything.

Night after night, day after day, year after year, the sexual and physical abuse continued. The only thing that would change would be who the predator was the next time.

At the young age of five, I prayed nightly for God to save me. Asking Him to send someone to love me seemed far-fetched at this point. Now, I prayed for someone to just protect me. I prayed to die at the hands of one of these monsters and end this cycle of hate and anger I was living in. However, the years went by, the torture went on and so did the mental, physical, and sexual abuse.

Dorm Life Continues

Everyone in the dorms had a few jobs. Mine was to serve the kids meals, clean up the mess, and make sure the tables and area were cleaned after chow. Since we were on a farm, everyone had to help tend to the animals, keep the dorms clean, help the other kids, go to chapel (yes, you read that right), and play in a sport.

It was a lot of work making the place look nice for the "organization organizers" to come and check out where they were donating money and items. Sadly, I looked forward to the days they were coming to visit. It meant we got to "play" like we were the poster facility with no skeletons lurking around. We got to "play" with the donated toys we got for Christmas we weren't usually allowed to play with. No rapes or beatings for a little while. Just a group of happy facilitators and kids being kids.

We were allowed visits from parents, guardians, and friends. I dreaded those days because I knew I would never have a visitor. Mother didn't put me up for adoption, she just left me there to rot. Holiday break would come, and some children would go home to their families while the rest of us "throw-away" kids would remain. Organizations would visit the kids left behind to play for the day and bring gifts to enjoy. That was great while they were here, but after they left, we were forced to give the toys back and go back to our miserable existence.

As I continued to pray for death or saving, a new spiritual battle started within me. After so much torture and hate from virtually everyone around me, I truly grew dark inside, and became numb to what was happening. I found myself trying not to become the monster I was being trained to become. The hate, bitterness, and anger just began to take over.

One evening as I returned to my room from another let's "chat in my room" meetings with a dorm parent, I prayed for God to save me or let me be killed. I was still too young to fight back, yet old enough to know there must be something better out there. After yet another night of praying fervently, but seeing no difference in my life, I vowed to God from that night on I would never ask Him for anything else as long as I lived.

This five-year-old-boy had seen unthinkable situations and been through unspeakable pain has had enough. I truly died that day and allowed my inner demons to protect me from then on. These kids and teachers would come to know me as a heartless, cold, soulless, bitter, and a very angry child. For years I watched many of my classmates go to insane asylums, kill themselves, or go back to their homes only to ruin their lives. As the cycle continued, I grew up believing that it was also my destiny and I accepted it.

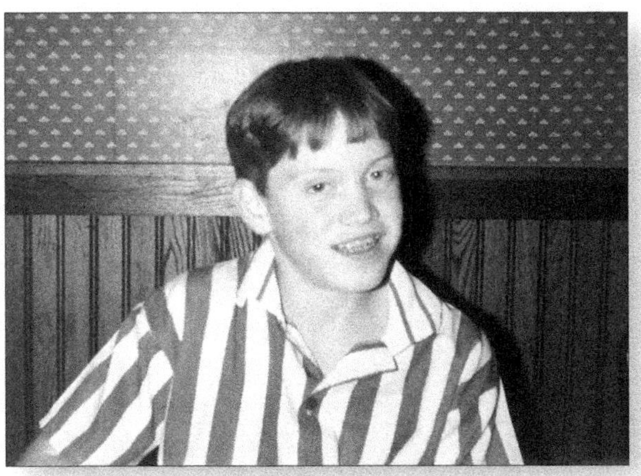

From ages five to thirteen, I grew bigger, angrier, and darker. I was going to become so big and so mean NO ONE would dare to mess with me again. Hate grew stronger, and bitterness ruled my every move. I just knew that one day I could snap. Everyone would soon know not to mess with me again.

THE DAY I SNAPPED

One of the older boys came to "mess" with us younger kids, again. I was close to thirteen years old at the time. I was done taking it! I took every ounce of hate and anger inside of me and decided to fight back. I had never fought back before. I didn't know how to fight. What I could do well, though was take a beating. I "blacked out" as I always did to "protect" myself. I decided I would let him tire himself out taking punch after punch. However, this time I kept getting back up, refusing to allow him to beat me again. He became exhausted within minutes. His punches were slowing, and he was starting to breath harder.

This was it. I saw my chance. I hit him with everything I had knocking him to the ground. I then got on top of him and started choking him. Still in the "black out" state, I held him until I felt his body go limp and he took his very last breathe. All the rage and anger had finally been unleashed. He just happened to be the one who felt all my pent-up anger.

When I "snapped out it," I looked up into the crowd that had formed around us. I saw everyone staring at me in fear. It was the way I looked at my "predators" all these years. They were looking at me in a whole new light. This is what I wanted though, right?

I didn't want to see myself become this. I didn't ask for this. This isn't who I wanted to become. They turned me into a monster like them. I now feared myself. I let go of his lifeless body, got up, and ran out the door. At that moment, I decided to run away and go anywhere but here.

NIKKI'S STORY BEGINS:

"The only person you are destined to become is the person you decide to be."

- Ralph Waldo Emerson[3]

[3] Pinterest.com

Chapter 3

MEANWHILE, IN INDIANA

IT WAS NOW 1983 and Nikki was about to be born into another dysfunctional American family. Her father beats her mother, gets drunk, says he's sorry, and does it again and again. Furthermore, he cheats, gets another woman pregnant, and finally her mother leaves. Sound familiar?

Pregnant with Nikki and one older daughter already, Nikki's mother moved them in with her grandmother. She did the best she could to provide for her family. When her mother found love again, she and the girls move in with her new love. For a while, life looked like it was going to turn out better for this family.

Nikki and her older Sister

Thankfully, it was a "safe" place, but over the years, it grew very loveless and cold. Her mother began to drink to cover the pain and her stepfather was gone a lot, finding reasons to work longer hours and be away from home.

For many years, the family went on just existing. There was no happiness, joy, fulfillment, or love. They just lived day-to-day as a dysfunctional ratrace family.

For this family, things started to turn darker around Nikki's tenth birthday. As her mother worked a little more each day and her stepfather was around less and less often, Nikki started acting out more and more. Trying to find love or attention anywhere she could, she found herself trying to fit in where she found acceptance. She began stealing cigarettes and taking a drink with the group she began to hang around with. Unfortunately, that was just the beginning.

Her drinking and cigarettes became less of a secret as time went on. By the age of thirteen, she was fully addicted to drugs, alcohol, and the party lifestyle. It seemed to help fill the void she was looking for, but only temporarily.

Then, her stepbrother died in a horrible car accident. Two weeks later, her grandmother died and then, two weeks after that, her parents filed for divorce. Things were spinning out of control all around her pushing her into a downward spiral, spinning out of control. Her drunken behavior and out of control attitude got her kicked out of the house. To add to her broken mess, she became homeless.

Thankfully, she had a lot of party "friends" who let her stay with them from time-to-time. She would go from party house to party house. She went from home to home when she could, but often found herself breaking into storage units to find a place to sleep. She often broke into her old house just to take showers before leaving for school.

She would go to school for shelter and safety. She would fill her Mickey-D cup with vodka to take to school with her every day to get herself through her day. Nikki would stay drunk all day. School was just a shelter for her, not a place to learn.

One evening, she was at one of her party friend's house, partying when an older gentleman noticed her. She had seen him around before and thought he was cute. She was excited someone like him wanted to talk to her. As the evening went on, Nikki got more intoxicated.

She and the guy started making out. This went on for some time before things became more heated. Things went farther than she expected. When she became uncomfortable with how far things were going, she tried to stop it from going any farther. At that point, the guy told her she can either participate or not, but it was going to happen. So, it happened.

Nikki went completely dark and bitter inside. From then on, she did everything she could to sabotage her life. She felt she had no reason to live, no reason to stay "pure," and no reason to think life would ever be different.

No one loved her.
No one wanted her except to use her.
She had nowhere to go, with no purpose at all.

Many nights, she would find herself walking around town drunk. She would pass out in a church parking lot or on a park bench all the time hoping someone, somewhere, somehow would find her and help her. It seemed everywhere she turned there was just another downward slide.

Suicidal thoughts constantly taunted her mind. She lived recklessly in hopes death would happen. She tried one evening to end her life by taking a whole bottle of Tylenol. She drank a fifth of vodka to wash all the pills down, wishing this would end the miserable existence she called "life." Instead, she had the worse stomach pain you could imagine. She told herself next time she tried to kill herself she would try a painless way.

Eventually, she wasn't satisfied with same drugs and alcohol she was using. It didn't stop the thoughts or cover the pain anymore. She was always trying to up the stakes. To others her age, it looked like she was living the teenage dream. Freedom to do whatever she wanted with no rules and no boundaries.

However, all she ever really wanted was for someone to love her and tell her she didn't need to live this way.
She longed for someone to tell her she had a purpose in life and she was meant for more than what her body could be used for.

Since this seemed like it would never happen, she just continued with her destructive lifestyle, always trying to push the limits. Living didn't matter to her, so if you told her she couldn't do it or shouldn't do it, she would always try to do it, not caring about the consequences.

Acid was introduced to her at a party one evening. Living in a "fake" reality was right up her alley. Never facing truth would be amazing, she thought. A new addiction started that night. Acid was now the "go to" drug for her. Though it was harder to find and expensive she sought it out.

Many nights, Nikki would hang out with her sister on the porch as she came down from her high. She promised her sister she would do better every time they talked. Though she vowed to do better and refrain from going on the acid trips, she didn't vow to stop everything else.

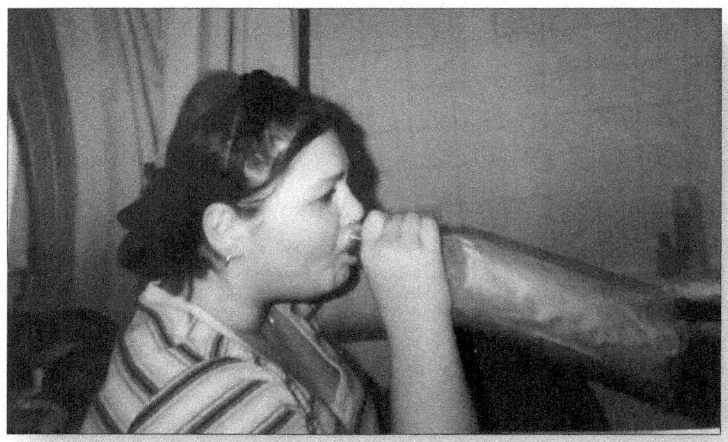

Nikki age 13

A new neighbor moved into the apartment building where Nikki was sleeping in the storage units. She soon found herself at a party filled with a much "older" crowd than she was used to. As she partied with them, they were impressed that this fourteen-year-old girl could drink most of them "under the table." She got a little too drunk and started getting loud and out of control. Since she was so young, the over-age crowd didn't want her to get caught there so they asked her to leave.

After drinking a whole fifth of Ever-clear mixed with Kool-Aid, she left. Never feeling "this" sick from being drunk, she felt as if she just needed to "sleep" it off. Unfortunately, being this drunk she couldn't find "home" or a place to go so she went into the laundry room of the apartments where her home was and ended up passed out behind the washer.

Two days passed since any one seen Nikki after that party. Some people searched for her but to no avail. People worried about what might have happened to her after she left that party.

The Last Straw

When Nikki woke up, she still felt sick, but didn't realize just how lucky she was she even woke up at all. She had passed out from alcohol poisoning. This was the last straw. She wanted a different life. So, she went back home to be with her mother and sister. Nikki begged her mother to let her stay there saying all she wanted was to be with her family again. Her mother agreed if she would agree to stop her drugs and drinking.

After over a year on the streets and having things "happen" that happen to drunken underage girls willing or not, Nikki was ready to return home and try to be the daughter her mother wanted her to be. They didn't know how to be a family, but she knew she didn't want to be alone anymore.

Nikki did well with this promise for a while. At fourteen, she was able to get her first job. She was trying to do better in school. She thought if she threw herself into a busier life, it would help keep her distracted.

Things came crumbling down just a short year later, but this time it was her sister who brought the family to its knees. We will have to skip those details because that is another book for another time. However, just know their family was forced to leave the place they were living and live in their car together. They also were forced into family counseling.

Thankfully, she had school and work to keep her busy and out of the car most of the time. Tight places and back seats still bother her today because of this time spent in the car. Living in the car together lasted about six months or so. Once her sister was admitted into a mental home, Nikki helped pay for a hotel room to get them out of the car for a while. The hotel became "home," though it still felt cold and loveless. At least they had a roof over their heads, and she was still sober. Nikki and her mom visited her sister from time to time. They would do their forced family counseling which made things a whole lot worse for them. Then they would go on about their miserable bleak lives.

She started dating and was doing well. Her sister came home from the hospital, and they once again tried the family thing. Sadly, the three of them together didn't work in long time frames. She found herself finding reasons to not be "home" again. She alternated staying with her new boyfriend, friends, and at home if no one else was there. She drifted back into just smoking weed, but kept her job, paying her half of the hotel, going to school, and staying on the "better" side of the road.

As she worked to stay on the "better" side of the road, life seemed to look a little better. Her mom and sister both started dating. She had dated the same guy for about two years now. Nikki, her boyfriend, her mother, and her mother's boyfriend all moved into an apartment together. The four of them had great relationships with each other and lived as "roommates" together for years to come.

She would go "clubbing" at underage dance clubs, smoke from time to time, hang out with friends drinking moderately, and doing better at school.

Things started to go better for this family. As the years went by, boyfriends changed, friends changed, and many friends passed away or went to jail.

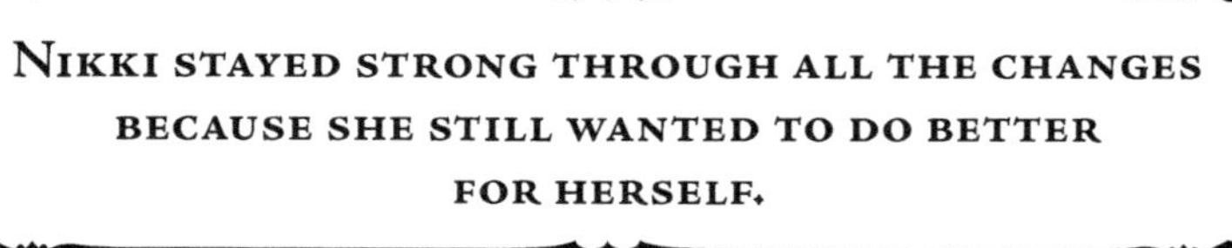

NIKKI STAYED STRONG THROUGH ALL THE CHANGES BECAUSE SHE STILL WANTED TO DO BETTER FOR HERSELF.

That is until Nikki had the most terrifying experience of her life at seventeen!

Robert's Story Continues:

“There are in nature neither rewards or punishments – there are consequences.

- Robert Ingersol[4]

[4] Goodreads.com

Chapter 4

BACK IN TEXAS

AFTER RUNNING AND hiding in the woods on the farm for a little while, I decided I would return and face my punishment. I declared I wouldn't let them win. I wouldn't allow myself to become one of them. I would face what I did and take whatever beating or jail sentence I deserved. Anything would be better than becoming one of them. They would never confess and live out whatever punishment they had coming.

I started walking back pondering what would happen. Jail would be awful, but it had to be better than it was here.

Once I reached the dorms, I stopped at the doorway, took a deep breath, and opened the door. As I walked down the hallway, I saw my dorm mates standing outside the infirmary. As I glanced in, to my complete amazement I saw the kid I choked to death laying there **awake**! He was beaten and broken but **alive**! How could this be?

The doctor said once he passed out, I let go and ran, Thankfully, he had just enough air still in him that once I let go and ran, his body stayed lifeless, but his lungs started to refill. He would soon go onto a full recovery.

I became known as the new monster on the block and someone you just didn't mess with anymore. I was now big enough and everyone was too afraid of me to mess with me, including the staff.

I stayed bitter and angry. It kept me going in this hell hole for the years to come. The years from fourteen to seventeen were less eventful. The boys' farms received new administration, new teachers, and new dorm parents over the years. I must say I am grateful to the last dorm parents I had here on the farm. They worked hard to break down my walls, though I could only let them in so close, I am thankful my time here will end with those dorm parents. The abuse got better for the newcomers, but us "old timers" would always remember.

Since Mom never put me up for adoption and just left me there to rot, I lived on the farm from age four to just about eighteen. When it was almost graduation and time to leave this place, I discovered leaving was harder than I thought.

When all you know is heartache and pain,
heartache and pain are all you seek.
It's comfortable, it's familiar.
The unknown and love become scary.

Robbie's Graduation

Graduation came and went. It was time to leave, but I didn't know what to do or where to go. I had many questions I wanted answered so, I decided to move to Arkansas where my mother was living with her new family for a little while. However, I didn't seem to fit into life there.

Mom had remarried, had a daughter who was now a teenager, and my older brother was living with her as well. I did enjoy getting to know my little sister. We seemed to have had an instant bond. My brother still seemed a little wary of me, but he did try to accept me. As I got to know my stepfather, I was happy he was a good man. He took care of his family. I was happy mom seemed to have found some peace in her life. I just didn't find my place among them. I did my best to work it out, but I just couldn't stay there.

Navy

So, I decided to join the Navy. The navy taught me a lot. I got to see a lot of amazing places. I became an electrician. I finally felt accomplished at something. Yet, I was still missing the love I had longed for my whole life. The Navy was amazing, but I basically went from one institution into another one. I still couldn't think for myself. I still didn't know how to be my own man or know who I truly was.

I got to travel to some beautiful places and met some truly amazing people along the way. Yet, I wanted something more. I decided to do my four years and move onto something else.

After I got out, I didn't know where to go or what to do so, I went back to the pain I knew and to what was familiar. Yes, I went back to the boys' farm to become a dorm parent. I wanted to be the dorm parent I wished I had while growing up there.

Unfortunately, that was short lived. Although I had come back to make a difference, the boys' farm was still a place of deep wounds for me. The man I was trying to become was going backward. It saddened me this place still could cut me to the core. I didn't like who I was there. I had to move on.

Where should I go to search for who I wanted to be?

So, I left in my pick-up truck and set out for the unknown.

Nikki's Story Continues:

"Everything you are experiencing today is a result of a decision you made in the past."
- Unknown[5]

[5] Goodreads.com

Chapter 5

NIKKI'S SCARIEST MOMENT

LIFE WENT ON for Nikki. Her sister and her mother both got married. Although, things went south with her boyfriend, she still went on with work and school. She became the manager at the food joint she had been working at for three years and enjoyed going out with friends and partying on a "smaller" social scale.

Although Nikki had not tried to commit suicide for a few years now, death still didn't bother her. Living this kind of lifestyle, she lost many of her friends. Some ended up in jail, some were killed dealing or taking drugs, others died in car accidents, some committed suicide, and some were killed. Although it never got easier, loss is what Nikki had already known too much about.

Nikki baby sat after school for a friend of hers from time to time to help her out. On one life-changing day, she had just dropped the baby off and was headed back home trying to avoid rush hour traffic.

While sitting at a red light, she saw a man run across the busy street, being chased by another man. The man started banging on car windows and trying to get into each of them shouting, "He is going to kill me!" Once the man got to her car, she unlocked the door and let him in, thinking she was doing the right thing.

Just as the light changed, the other guy got in a car behind them. The guy in her car started screaming for her to go and lose the car behind them. The guy in the car yelled at her and told her where to turn. He said the other guy had a gun and she needed to keep turning left, that way if the guy behind them was going to shoot they would shoot her.

After some time of this crazy driving, it looked like they finally lost the car behind them. As they got a little distance away from the neighborhood, Nikki asked the man to get out since he was now safe. He said no they were still not safe, and she needed to keep driving. As she drove, the man continued to panic. Being afraid for her life, she knew they were coming to a busy intersection, and it was rush hour. She pushed the gas pedal down and prayed to be hit by a car as they flew into the intersection. Cars screeched to swerve and miss her car. She didn't know what to do, or what was going to happen to her once they could stop, so she did just as he said. As he had her continued to drive, they heard a radio blast of a kidnapping. It was a description of her car being sent out over the broadcast. That caused the man to panic even more. In his panic, he started throwing his stuff all around in her car.

As they approached the next busy intersection, they could see it was completely blocked by police cars. More cops came up behind them and blocked her car in between the two intersections. Now with nowhere to go and nowhere to hide, she wondered what this man would do. She feared it could turn into a hostage situation. She didn't know what to do, so she stopped the car in the middle of the two intersections.

The cops drew their weapons and began to close in on her car. As they approached the car, the man finished throwing his stuff all around the car. Then, he told her to tell them his name was Bob, and finally sat calmly.

When the cops reached the car no words where to be said. They had guns drawn, yelling for them to get out of the car with their hands up. Without saying anything to the man now sitting calmly in her car, Nikki immediately did as they commanded.

The police threw Nikki onto her car and read her rights as he handcuffed her. As she looked over the top of the police car, she watched them force the man out of her car. Nikki did everything the cops asked her, but in fear she said, "Take me anywhere you want as long as it's away from that man."

The cop asked, "Why?"

She proceeded to tell him she didn't know the man, how he got in her car, told her what to do, and refused to get out when she asked him to, so she kept doing as he said. The cops then changed how they treated her. The police called for victim assistance as well as Nikki's family to come to the scene since she was a minor. Once her stepdad showed up, the cops told them to stay at the scene until victim assistance showed up.

After a few hours, everyone but one officer had left. Nikki and her stepdad waited with the officer for three hours for the victim assistance lady to show up! The lady didn't even get out of her car once she finally arrived! The lady handed her some pamphlets through the window of her car as she told Nikki to read them and if she had any questions to call her, her name was on the back. Nikki thought to herself, we waited all this time for that! It was so not helpful!

Reality of what could have happened had not fully set in. As they pulled up to the house, they saw news crews had shown up on her doorstep and wanted the story from her. She just wanted to move on and forget the whole thing.

The next day is when reality and all the drama set in. When she got to school, everyone knew what had happened. Everyone was asking questions. They were all hugging her as if they actually cared. The news crews were there, too. It seemed news crews were everywhere she turned.

The morning after returning to school, she woke up to find all four of her car tires slashed. She got a ride to school wondering why. What did she do? When she gets to school, she found out some of the man's family go to school there.

Constant threats were made against her saying if she pressed charges against the man, she would have hell to pay. Little did they know the state pressed charges not her. She had no control; she was the victim in the situation.

Nikki had two weeks left of high school! The threats made at school, the constant tire slashing, and the stares from people in public made it difficult for her to leave her house. She had a meeting with the school, and they insured her safety to get her through the last two weeks. If she agreed to show up, she would graduate with her friends. So, for the next two weeks, she only left the house to go to school and then came right back home. Thankfully, she graduated with her class.

Graduation Nikki & Her Sister

Afterwards though, fear overwhelmed her, and she decided not to leave her house again during the daylight hours. She went into a deeper depression than she had ever known. She ate and slept while doing hardly anything else. She soon found herself weighing over 300 pounds. She was miserable again with her life and herself.

Everything she had worked so hard for was gone. She tried going out from time to time to party with close friends, but only at night and only with people she knew. Nikki's sister moved into the apartments next door and that's when the partying really started up again. She finally had a place close to home where she could go and feel safe.

She fell back into old habits and began drinking more and more. Ecstasy was the new drug around and she used it to try to lose touch with reality once again.

Drugs took over again for the next few years. The depression, fear, and anxiety Nikki felt was just unbearable.

The kidnapping trial took years to complete. She was forced to relive those moments, being treated by the other lawyer as if she had done something wrong.

She was questioned daily and had the prosecutor pick her apart as a person trying to get this man off. Having the jury look at her trying to see if she was lying or telling the truth made her anxiety worse and more afraid of people seeing her in public.

The trial finally ended, and the man was sentenced to 33 1/2 years with multiple charges against him. By the time the trial ended, Nikki was nineteen years old. The depression, fear, and anxiety now ruled her every thought as well as her life.

At twenty, something snapped inside, and she decided she wasn't going to live in fear like this anymore. She got a job working on a military post. She felt safe working there due to the security set in place. She fought to stay drug free and deal with her depression and fears head on.

This job was amazing for her. It helped to bring her slowly out of her depression. This job gave her purpose. She started moving up in the ranks quickly. Soon, she was a team leader and doing well for herself. She started dating again and working on improving herself! A few years went by, and life smoothed out for a little while.

However, Nikki knew all good things must come to an end.
She was just waiting for the other shoe to drop.
It came just three years later.

"The best way to find yourself
is to lose yourself in the service of others."
- Mahatma Gandhi

"To find yourself, think for yourself."
- Socrates

Chapter 6

Finding Ourselves

Robert's Story
What Happened After I Left Texas

AFTER I LEFT Texas, I worked various odd jobs. I worked in the oil fields, as a librarian, I delivered furniture, I was a bread maker, as well as a security guard. I lived in my truck for many years. Living off peanut butter and bread slices with my only possession being a single plate.

I decided to change careers from being an electrician. When I moved to Oklahoma, I went back to school for my A&P license. I went to school during the day, worked at night, slept in the truck, and showered in truck stops. Life was hard, but it had always been hard for me.

The difference was I was becoming who I chose to be not who I was trained to be. Even though I had nothing, I wasn't afraid for my life. I was finally finding me. I was finding who I could become when I let my guard down. Dating became an experiment to see what kind of girls I liked. I will never forget this one date. I saved up money for weeks to take this girl on a date. We went out to a fancy restaurant. This girl ate hardly anything. She just took a few bites here and there.

She said, "I'm just not to hungry."

I didn't know how to react to this. After saving for weeks to take her out, I wasn't going to let her food go to waste.

I had them box up the leftovers and I took it home for lunch the next day. I dropped her off, said goodnight and drove off. I got a few blocks down the road when I realized she still had my jacket on. Of course, I turned back to get it, knocked on the door, and her father answered.

Her father said, "Boy, I thought you took my daughter out to eat."

I was taken back by his statement, "I did sir, but she said she wasn't hungry."

He let me in and led me to the kitchen. I found his daughter standing in the fridge doorway stuffing her face from the dinner her parents had left over. She was shoveling it down!

I told myself I would not do that ever again. We did have one more date, but it was at Taco Bell. I ordered her one taco at a time! After that I decided I would hold off on looking for love a little longer. I told her we were just not a good fit for each other.

I finished A&P school, took a job in Georgia, and got an apartment. For the first time in a long time, I started collecting personal items. I finally had more than just a plate. Life was lonely but it was my life. I would date from time to time. As I got comfortable with a girl, I would start to tell her **some** of my past. Each time, the girl would react the same. They would cry, feel pity for me, and look at me like after all I'd been through, I had to be crazy. I didn't want any of that. What I wanted was for people to see they can choose who they want to be and break the cycle of family curses.

Yes, I am broken, and I do have a few "triggers" from (undiagnosed) PTSD. Yes, loving is hard for me since I never knew it, but caring isn't.

I didn't want pity, I wanted someone who would understand, come along side me, but not try to "fix" me. I worked hard daily to earn the things I had and carefully chose who I wanted to have in my life. My circle of friends is small, I was careful about who I let in.

As I reached my 30s,
I continued to build and tweak who
I wanted to be.
I grew to know myself.
Finally, I stopped caring about what others
thought of me.

Nikki's Story

Get Out of Town

Nikki was now into her 20s. Her sister had given custody of her two children to their mother. Nikki agreed to help financially take care of them since she couldn't take physical care of them. She was a manager on the contracting job by day and manager of a restaurant at night. Working on herself, paying bills, and focusing on staying sober, she was very busy.

Things were about to change starting with a phone call one night as she was leaving her night job. It was very strange. The person on the other end of the line started off by telling her he was watching her. He described everything she was wearing, the people she was with, and said he wanted to let her know he was watching. It really creeped her out, but she felt as though maybe one of her friends was pulling a prank on her. Although she felt uneasy, she shrugged it off and continued with her evening.

A few days went by, and she received another call. Close to the same as before, but this time he let her know he knew where she lived and described the house and her family including the kids. A little more spooked this time, she didn't know what to do, but sleeping that night wasn't easy.

The calls became less frequent, but consistently more violent with each call. The man started telling her how he would kill her and her family. How he would make her watch her nieces die before he killed her. Each call was a little more thought out than the previous one, too.

Nikki didn't know who this was and didn't know why she was being targeted. The fear and anxiety she fought so hard to overcome returned. She started wanting to hide inside and return to drugs and alcohol to make it fade away. The fear of the people in this world was resurfacing. The difference was this time she had the two girls to help feed. She couldn't just hide at home. She had to fight to keep going to work and face the world even though she just wanted to hide.

One day, Nikki and some friends were able to trace the number back to an address. She was tired of looking over her shoulder all the time and fearing she was putting the kids in danger. Nikki and a friend went to this home. She boldly knocked on the door as her friend stood off to the side to "catch him off guard as he answered." They heard the person come to the door but not open it or answer.

Nikki started yelling through the door, "I'm tired of hiding and just waiting to see what you will do! I am right here! If you're going to kill me, kill me now! Come on, open the door and take your shot at me. Now that I'm here, you want to hide behind a door!"

Since the man didn't answer, Nikki decided to call the police. She explained where she was as well as the situation, and how this man was making threatening phone calls to her.

The lady from the police department said, "I will send police there but just know that you are trespassing on his property now. You may be questioned for stalking him!"

Scared now she would be the one going to jail, she hung up the phone and drove away as quickly as she could. Facing her fear head on seemed to have worked. No calls happened for a while.

Nikki went back to life as she knew it. Working all the time and trying to keep moving forward even though she felt she might never get the answers.

Who has been threatening her?

Nikki began to find herself sabotaging relationships mainly because she didn't feel worthy. Secondly, she didn't want to bring anyone else too close into her crazy world and put someone else's life in danger. She dated men she felt she could focus on fixing their problems instead of focusing on hers. Doing this made her feel like she was doing something good for someone else.

As life would have it, she received a reminder call to let her know he was still watching! She had no clue why he was watching her! One day, she decided to get an update on the man who was in jail because of her testimony against him. Just as she feared the site said released! It had only been 3.5 years! *Good behavior shaves that much time off? Could this be him? she thought.*

She called the victim assistance to get answers. After some chasing people down with many hours on the phone, they let her know he had appealed the case. Nikki failed to appear in court, so all charges were dropped. He was released with time served!

Nikki was completely overwhelmed. Floored by what she found out! Every emotion you could possibly imagine flooded through her within seconds.

Why didn't she get the subpoena?
Why did the system fail to protect her?
Was this revenge?
Was he going for her to set the record straight?
Was he the one behind it all?
Could anything be done?

Calling the police station and asking lawyers gave her the same answer, "No." They said, "A call is just a call. No proof of who it was or that they will ever do as they threaten. No face, so there can be no lawsuit. No lines were being crossed, and no laws were broken."

Frustrated, but deciding life must go on, she had to try to keep moving forward and not allow this man to take her life away from her again. Nikki decided to try dating again. This time she seems to have found a good man. He stood by her side as she fought her depression and her fears as hard as she could. He tried to help her through them, making her see she was worth loving. He advised her not to run when she told him about the calls or threats. He tried to make her feel as safe as he could.

Things got serious quickly between them. Nikki wanted things to work out this time, so she focused on work, helping with kids, and doing the best she could to pull herself out of this depression.

After some time had passed, he called again! This time he said if she left town, he would leave her family alone. He wouldn't touch the kids or ever call again. He wouldn't call again if she would just leave his town. The next few calls were similar.

Nikki would have her chance to leave soon. Her now fiancé got a new position in Georgia. Her job was starting a new contract at the same location he where he was going to be! Knowing this was the best choice for her to save her family and have a new start herself,

NIKKI LEFT FOR HER NEW LIFE FULL OF HOPE IN GEORGIA.

GEORGIA DOESN'T SEEM MUCH DIFFERENT

When Nikki got to Georgia, she told herself she would be the person she always wanted to be. She would leave the old her and her old life behind her. She would find herself, start over, and focus on her new life.

She never had dreams or hopes before. "Why bother," she thought, "life would always take her out when she tried, so what was the point."

Now, she found herself with the opportunity to try new things and find what she liked and didn't like. It was her time to find herself.

Unfortunately, on her road to finding herself, she left the man she moved with to Georgia. She told him she wanted to go on the journey to find herself alone with no roadblocks.

It was a humbling experience as she sought to find a place to live by herself. Her "new" place to call home was an old, rundown trailer only costing $400 a month including all utilities. Mice would eat the little bit of food she fought so hard to bring home. The snakes living in the walls would then kill the mice. It was the circle of life all around her, but she made the most of it.

She started going to beauty school to pursue what she thought would be a cool job as a horror movie makeup artist. She started working out twice a day and lost 150 pounds. She gained a confidence she never had before. She found her voice and her strength. Fighting hard to overcome her past, she came out of her depression and became proud of who she was now becoming.

Nikki's first home on her own

However, she soon found Georgia wasn't too different. She found a job but soon her new boss started assaulting her because she refused to have sex with him. She stood her ground. Like other men in power she had known, her boss didn't like it when he didn't get his way. She'd had enough of people using her, so she endured the assaults from her boss. She tried to find ways not to be around him alone. However, the "boss" had the power to send people home if he wanted to get her alone and assault her. She felt she had to keep this job so she could continue sending money home for her nieces.

Going to beauty school, working long hours, and getting assaulted became too much for her to handle alone. She had an emotional break down one day while she was at the school. Later in the afternoon, her classmate found her crying in the massage room, and never left her side while she wept for several hours. This was the beginning of her first friendship in Georgia.

She realized she had to find a new job. She refused to allow this man to take her down the path she had walked away from to create a new life for herself. At the same time, she decided she couldn't fight these battles alone anymore. She went to a local church recommended to her and found where she needed to be. She would go every time the doors were open and found herself crying in the back row at every service. She just wanted to be redeemed from her past.

Sunday came and like clockwork she went to the service. The altar call came as it always did, but this one would be different. Her heart started racing. She grew hotter as they kept praying. She felt a push from within to go up to the altar. Not feeling worthy or ready to except Christ, she left the church.

She got in the car telling herself she would be ready one day, but today just wasn't it. When she tried to start the car, it wouldn't start! This happened often so she kept trying, to no avail.

She looked up to the sky as she shouted out loud, "Really?"

She walked back into the church with the intention of sitting in the back row, and waiting until the service ended, so she could ask someone for help. Instead, she found herself walking straight up to the altar. Many people surrounded her and started praying over her and laying hands on her. She received Christ in her heart that day.

It would be awesome if I could say her car started after service, but it was down for the count. She threw herself into God. Soaking up all the classes and studies she could, trying to fill the God-shaped hole in her heart. She started taking the "Making peace with my past" class the church was offering. This class was an amazing turning point in Nikki's life. She followed the class and did every exercise in the book to help her allow God to set her free.

Indiana

One evening, Nikki received a call from Indiana saying her "uncle" who she called "Dad" was sick. He was not going to live much longer. She decided it was time for her to go back home and be with family. She was stronger now. She was a different person. She was sober and happy with who she'd become. With God on her side, she was ready to face Indiana again. She packed up and prepared to move all her things back to Indiana.

Our Journey Begins:

"Joy is what happens when we allow ourselves
to recognize how good things are.
Joy is what happens when we see God's plan is perfect
and we are already starring in a perfect show.
- Marianne Williamson[6]

[6] Goodreads

Chapter 7

Robert: The Beginning of Us

NOW THAT I have been in Georgia for a few years and am truly happy with who I am, I decided to try one more time to find someone whom I may be able to share my time with. One day while getting a haircut, I asked my barber if she happened to have any single friends.

She said, "As a matter of a fact I do."

She handed me a piece of paper with a name and a number on it. I kept the paper for a few days pondering when would be a good time to call and what to say. I finally said, "what the hell" and called, "what is the worst that could happen?"

You guessed it! Nikki was the best friend my barber set me up with on a blind date. When I introduced myself to Nikki, I introduced myself as "Anthony." I had decided the next women I would meet I would be who I wanted to be. Going by my middle name would give me a chance to truly start over as a whole "new" person.

Nikki was skeptical about meeting me since she knew she was moving to Indiana soon. Instead of meeting right away, we texted and called back and forth for two weeks.

I was already pleased with who I was getting to know just by phone. I hadn't laid eyes on her yet, but she was already so beautiful inside. I convinced her to meet me before leaving for Indy. Neither one of us expected this blind date to change our lives forever.

Nikki was stunning. Knocked me off my feet from the first moment I laid eyes on her. She had such a radiant glow and a confidence like I had never seen. It was as if my soul knew right away, she was going to be the one.

We went to dinner at this little Mexican restaurant just down from my place. Nikki and I talked there for hours. It was so easy to talk to her. We just talked and laughed. Neither of us wanted the night to end, but the restaurant was closing soon.

We went back to my place. I had decided to turn on a cartoon to lighten the mood, so she didn't think I was going to attempt anything. We continued our conversation from dinner. After several more hours just laughing and talking, Nikki started opening up to me about how she was doing in her "making peace with her past" class. She briefly shared a small story about how she had some skeletons she was dealing with and how she was learning to deal with her past in a different manner.

This opened the door for me to share a small portion of my story with her. As I told her a few of my testimonies for the first time ever, she didn't look at me in fear. She didn't feel sorry for me. She didn't look at me like I must be crazy. She looked at me with complete understanding knowing how hard it is to overcome and do your best daily not to be the person you were trained to be.

It was absolutely astounding. I finally found the one person in the world who finally understood me. Now it was up to me not to be my awkward self and screw this up! She was amazing. It took every ounce of strength I had not to grab and kiss her the entire evening. She was everything I had searched for my whole life.

It got very late. I walked her to her car. I swear I was trying to remain the perfect gentleman, but it was hard holding back. We talked a little more after she started to get in the car. While standing outside of the car, we agreed to meet again the next evening. I moved closer as she seemed to lean in. My mind told me to keep it at the kiss on the cheek, but my heart longed for this moment. To find someone as incredible as her, I couldn't end this evening with any regrets, so I followed my heart.

I put my arm over her shoulder onto the car. I leaned in and waited for her response. She leaned in the rest of the way. I had never known a kiss like hers. I can't even put into words how I felt. My mind had been blown by this woman. I must admit I was completely captivated.

The next night, we met again on River Street in Savannah. We had some desserts and enjoyed all the shops and vendors Savannah had to offer. We rested on a bench to enjoy each other's company while looking over the Savannah River. We listened to music from the local restaurant across the way.

A gentleman approached us as we sat on the bench. He asked if he could make a pretty rose for the pretty lady. I agreed because I knew it would be a great addition to our evening. He stood next to us as he made a rose from Palm Frond. It was neat watching him make it in front us. As he made it, he started to "prophetically" speak over us. The gentleman told us, "Y'all are going to make it, I can just tell. Y'all will be married within two years and have twins."

I told him we would see because it was only our second date.

The man said, "Well, y'all got it and I can see it. Take my word y'all will marry with children soon."

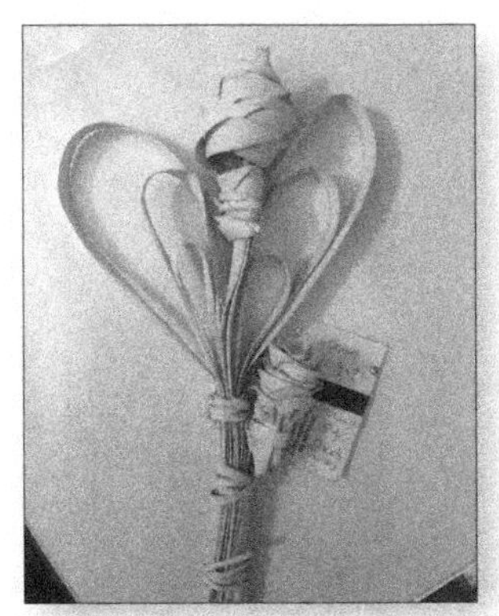

The Palm Frond Rose

I took the rose and gave it to Nikki. She smiled. We wrote the man's name down along with what he had told us and kept the paper with the rose. We just laughed off what the man said, though, and went on to continue our evening together.

It was as if our souls had known each other our whole lives. We just complemented each other so well. For the first time in both of our lives, we were being who we wanted to be. The best part was we both enjoyed being completely free as well as completely honest with one another.

For the two weeks Nikki had left to stay in Georgia, we were inseparable. We saw each other every day, even if it would be for just a short lunch break together. We talked and text all throughout the day.

Every chance we had, we went into Savannah and played tourist. We saw the town in ways we had never seen it before. We went to the museums, the old forts, and some iconic places around Savannah. Even though I'd seen these places before, being with her made it all seem so new to me.

The way I looked at life was changing. Opening to love had always been scary, but with her it wasn't scary at all. It felt so easy and natural.

Her best friend's wedding day was quickly approaching. Knowing she would be gone soon was unbearable. Every time we saw each other, I would ask her to stay. I didn't want to seem desperate, but I couldn't imagine letting her go without knowing what could be! I knew she was the one for me, but how was I to get her to see it and feel it as I did.

Robert and Nikki dolphin tour

Nikki called home one day and was telling her "Uncle/Dad" about this amazing man she'd met. She said he was firm yet kind, gentle yet rugged, caring and understanding yet as broken as she was. He was very attentive and very attractive. He wasn't intimidated by her crazy fears and quirks. He understood her completely. He didn't fear trying to break through the rough exterior wall she had built by taking one brick down at a time, instead of being a wrecking ball. She told him, the man she had met could be the one, but she was torn about not being there for her family when they needed her.

Her "Dad" told her, "Nikki, I'm gonna die whether you come home or not. If you are gonna have the slightest 'should've, could've, would've' about this man, please don't come home. Stay there and see how it goes with him."

Nikki decided to stay in Georgia, but kept it to herself for the moment.

A Night to Remember

On her best friend's wedding day, I was to share it with her as her date. Yet, I knew she would be gone in just a matter of days. I decided I wouldn't ask her again to stay, I would just enjoy every minute we had together.

Best Friend's Wedding

We danced, laughed, and had the greatest night you could imagine. We enjoyed making memories with the friends around us, but for most of the evening, to me it seemed as if it was just the two of us. Every time I looked at her, I longed for her to stay. Her beauty and essence had me completely in love with her. The thought of love had terrified me, until I met Nikki.

As the night was ending, I invited Nikki to come back to the hotel I was staying at close to the wedding location. I just didn't want the night to end. When I held her in my arms it was as if I was holding on to an angel. I enjoyed who I was when I was around her. Not having to hide my background, and not having to fear she would think I was crazy if I told her my fears and the nightmares I still dealt with was so refreshing. I could be 100 percent myself for the first time and it was so freeing. Even though I didn't know how to love, I knew I would spend every day of my life trying to show her.

My intentions were pure(ish). I just wanted to stay close to her. When she was with me, it was as if my life had meaning and purpose. We talked and held each other for a while recapping the fun of the evening. Then passion set in…let's just say it was night I won't forget.

After our amazing night together, Nikki came over to visit on Monday evening with a gift bag for me. I was nervous. I figured it was a parting gift because she was to leave on Saturday.

When I nervously looked inside, there were a few little items hiding under the lining on top. Nikki instructed me to take each one out one by one so she could explain what it meant.

The first item I took out was a picture of us from our date on the sunset dolphin cruise. Nikki said, "That is so you can remember all the fun we had together, and you can see my face whenever you wanted." I was sure now this was a goodbye bag. Her excitement for me to keep going is what kept me going because inside I was so saddened by her leaving.

The second item I took out of the bag was a keychain heart. Nikki said, "This is because you have completely won my heart over. I am so blessed to have been able to share these past few weeks with you. You have opened my heart up, and I love you." Oh, the words I have been so terrified to ever hear just come out of her mouth! I loved her so much already. Though I was terrified of the thought of learning how to love, I was ready to try to show the love I felt even though I didn't know how.

As she looked at me nervously to see what I would say next, she told me to hold my thoughts and keep going. Next, I grabbed a key. Nikki said, "That is the key to my storage unit in Indiana where all of my things are." As I looked at her confused, she told me to keep going.

Then, I took out a business card to a local barbershop in town, with her name written on it. I looked up at her and I said, "Does this mean what I think it means?" She smiled so big and said, "Yes, it means I took a job here. I am going to stay here to see where this relationship goes. I talked to Dad, and he said if I had any doubts about leaving before I had seen how this would go, then I was not to leave. I really do want to see where this goes! The key is because we will have to take a trip to Indy soon to gather my things and you can meet my dad."

Could this really be happening? I have never been so overjoyed and filled with such emotion and love in my life! I didn't know what love looked like, but I sure knew what it didn't look like. I was determined to show her daily how much she meant to me. She was the one and I knew it. I wasn't going to let her get away.

Nikki and I became inseparable. We were living in our own little bubble. Both of us were finally freed from the pressure of our pasts because we were able to be open with one another about all our short comings and fears the past had left on us. Both of us were comfortable with who we were both inside and outside, and finding ourselves 100 percent happy for the first time in both of our lives.

Unexpected News

Three weeks had passed since Nikki decided to stay. I called her on my lunch as I always did just to hear her voice. When she answered she seemed a little distracted. I asked her if she was okay, and she said she didn't feel very good. That she had some irregular bleeding and was going to go to the doctor. I asked if she wanted me to go with her, but she politely said no, she would let me know how it went.

The next day, Nikki went to the doctor to make sure everything was okay. She took a pregnancy test as part of the routine at the doctor's office and thought nothing more of it.

When the doctor come in, he said, "Congratulations on your pregnancy!"

Nikki was stunned, scared, and in total disbelief. All these emotions overtook her at once. She began to weep.

The doctors said, "Is this not a good thing?"

She didn't know if it was or not! She was always told she couldn't have kids do to past medical issues. We had talked about how we both felt about kids. Both of us agreed to have no kids. Now, here we were pregnant.

Nikki left the office and called her mother. Crying and unsure of what to say to me. Nikki feared losing the baby, making me angry, how she would be as a mother, what would happen if I didn't want to raise the baby, and so on. Her mother calmed her down and told her it would be okay.

Her mother stated to her, "After you tell him you're pregnant, if he wants nothing to do with you, then you can come home as you once planned since you haven't been here to get your stuff yet. We will deal with it."

Terrified, Nikki called me to ask if we could talk about what the doctor said. I told her my lunch was coming up and we could meet for lunch. We agreed to meet at Chick Fil A just down the road from my work.

I could tell she had been crying. I feared she had bad news about the results. I was prepared to help her through whatever she needed. We are a team now. We could get through anything. Nikki insisted we sit outside first before we went into order.

I said, "Nikki, what is wrong? Tell me? It's okay, we will get through it together."

Nikki took something out of her purse, slammed her hand on table, started to cry, and cried out, "You knocked me up!"

As I tried to wrap my head around what she just said, she rambled on hysterically, "I know we only slept together once, but it is yours. You don't have to stay with me if you don't want to. We will go back to Indy, and you never have to hear from us again. I know we talked, and we didn't want kids. I'm sorry I didn't mean for this to happen."

Clearly, she just rambled on in fear.

I shouted, "Stop, please, and let me process it for a second. First, you are not going anywhere or moving with my child. Second, I love you. Though we didn't want children, we will raise this child together."

I got up and sat next to her. We just sat outside the restaurant embracing for a little while until she calmed down.

I told her, "We will figure it out."

Though I seemed calm on the outside to help ease her fears, I was screaming if fear on the inside. We didn't have a lot, but what we did have was love. I kept asking myself…

> *How was I going to provide for her?*
> *How was I going to be as a father?*
> *I worked so hard to be a better man, will I turn out to be like my father?*
> *Do I only had enough love in my heart for Nikki, could I love another as much as her?*
> *How am I to raise a child? I don't know what a "good home" looks like.*

Anxiety began to take over as I returned to work. My boss is one of my closest friends. I told him I just found out I was going to be a dad.

He patted me on the back and said, "I'm proud of you, Robby, for finally opening your heart and your life to love. Now, you two will be complete. I know you will be an amazing father because you are an amazing man."

I tried to keep focused on work for the day, but how could I? I asked to leave for the day so I could go be with Nikki.

Together we sat on her couch. We held each other in silence as we tried to figure out what to say to one another. We shared everything up to this point about our fears and failures, so why not put it out there now, I thought.

After sitting for a while, I looked at her and said, "Nikki, this isn't how we planned it, but it was meant to be this way. I love you. I am so nervous and fearful about the type of father I will be. How will I take care of our child and you? But I do know I have never loved anyone before you. I know if I'm going to be a father, I only would want it with you. We will figure out how to love and be good parents together. One mistake at a time. One daily choice to do better. We have each other now, which is more than we have ever had. We can conquer anything together."

Since we were pregnant and she was higher risk, we decided to move in together. It would save money, and I could be there any time she needed me. The friends Nikki had been staying with had moved into their new home, so it only made sense for me to leave my apartment. I would stay with her at the house she was living in because it had bigger space.

How could I get so lucky? I get to wake up next to this beauty every morning. I get to be there for her if she ever needs me. I was ready to start this new life with her and our child.

We Are Pregnant

"Today I affirm:
I am blessed.
I am powerful.
I am light.
I am highly favored.
I am more than a conqueror.
I am walking in purpose.
I am a child of the Most High God."
- Germany Kent[7]

---

[7] Goodreads.com

Chapter 8

THE PREGNANCY

AFTER THE INITIAL shock and fear wore off, we began to get really excited about the pregnancy. Because of some medical problems, Nikki was at higher risk of a miscarriage. After some medical advice and much consideration, we decided to go with a midwife and have a water birth.

At the midwife center, they provided monthly classes to help prepare you as a couple for what was to come with every month. Since we knew nothing at all about pregnancy, the body changes, or what to expect, this proved to be a great assist for Nikki and me.

They have videos to help the fathers understand what it was like for the women. They had classes in how to take the baby's vitals, swaddling, importance of skin-to-skin contact, and so much more. We really enjoyed our experience at every class.

With the first ultrasound coming up, we were so excited. We went to lunch after most classes to discuss what we each learned. Then, we got onto the subject of whether we thought it would be a boy or girl.

I suddenly remembered what the gentleman said to us on our second date! I said, "What if what the man said was true and it is twins! My mom is a twin so it's possible."

Nikki looked at me horrified it could be true.

"Oh no, we aren't speaking it into existence!" she exclaimed.

With the thought in both of our minds, we couldn't wait to see what was in store at the ultrasound, one or two?

Our First Ultrasound

It felt like our first ultrasound took months to get here! On the way to get the ultrasound, we joked a lot about if we had a girl, I would be wrapped around her finger. If she was half as amazing as her mother, I would be. Nikki and I both wanted a boy. The thought of having a girl terrified us both. The thought of twins was even scarer.

We knew knowing the gender was still many weeks away, so we returned our focus to the ultrasound we had today. We were just so overwhelmed with joy to get to see the baby for the first time.

The lady came into the room, asked what seemed like million questions then said "Okay, let's see what we can find."

I was a nervous wreck. Nikki seemed calm, but I'm sure her heart was racing just as fast as mine was.

The technician scanned over the baby, "Everything looks great this baby is…" and she went on talking about the measurements, the weeks, and how everything looked great here.

I was so overwhelmed with a million emotions. Excitement, fear, joy, love, and anxiety all at the same time. Seeing my baby on the screen, the reality of this happening, and the little pea I created was amazing. Seeing a life, I am now responsible for and raise as I shared this responsibility with the most amazing woman I have ever met filled my heart with joy. My thoughts were going a million miles an hour inside my head.

Then, she spoke the words, "And baby B over here" …Wait, come again?

She stated, "You are having twins and baby B looks great as well."

Nikki and I looked at each other. The best we could do was laugh at each other's reaction. We knew it was possible, but now it was reality. How are we going to do this?

We finished at the center got into the car, again not knowing what to really say. We both just sat staring out the window in disbelief.

With a nervous giggle Nikki said, "Well, looks like the man was right, I guess it's going to be one boy and one girl for us!"

"Hopefully, they come out as ginger as you," Nikki stated.

"Hopefully, they are as beautiful as you. I am thankful they are both healthy and at size. We will figure the rest out as it comes."

Nothing we could really do but except the fact it was twins. We were expanding our family quickly and finishing the expansion all at the same time.

With Nikki and I now expecting twins, we needed a bigger space than the house we were staying in would allow. We started the hunt for a new place to live and to raise our family. The process was long.

Thankfully, since we were first time home buyers, and I was prior military, we were able to secure a loan with no money down. We finally found the perfect starter home. It was nestled in a small town, with a fenced in yard, and three bedrooms with a den for a playroom. It was perfect for us.

I never knew my life would be this amazing. Only in my dreams did I think a love and life like this would be possible. I woke up every morning and reminded myself to show her how much I love her. I wanted her to know how grateful I was to have found her and to share my life with her. Though I might not be able to offer her much, I would offer to earn her love every day and give our family a safe home. I knew I could be the man I wanted to be for my family, I just had to try daily to earn them.

We finally made the move. The pregnancy was going well, and life just couldn't get better. We both continued to work full time. We started putting away money for Nikki's maternity leave. When Nikki was halfway through the pregnancy, we would be able to find out the genders.

The week before our appointment, I received a call my mother was very ill. She might not survive the surgery to be performed immediately. The family asked me to come and be there with them at this time. Nikki and I agreed it would be important for me to be there for her and to see the family.

So, I flew to Arkansas to be with my family. Though we weren't very close, Nikki and I wanted to try to mend these relationships with our families in hopes our children would have the opportunity to have "family" in their lives. We thought this would be a great first step.

However, I felt horrible I couldn't go to the ultrasound with Nikki. It was ripping my heart out she had to go alone, but she assured me it would be okay. She would surprise me with the genders when I got back.

Our Second Ultrasound

Nikki went into the ultrasound appointment excited to video tape it for me. She turned on the camera and focused in on the screen. They found baby A. All measurements looked great. Development was looking good. Then the technician said those beautiful words, "It's a boy." Nikki smiled from ear to ear. She was grateful we would have our boy.

She was excited to see if it would be two boys or if we would have the baby girl as well. The technician searched for baby B. Once B was located, she really didn't say as much as she did before. She just said, "There's B." The technician stated the fun part was over and Nikki could turn the camera off. Nikki questioned her statement since she still didn't know what baby B was, but she did as instructed. The technician then told Nikki baby B had lost its heartbeat. Baby B didn't develop like baby A did. The technician told her it was common with twins and baby A would be fine.

Devastated, Nikki left the appointment. She wondered how she could keep this to herself. How could she act happy when I called her to see how it went? What did she do to make this happen? How was she supposed to protect the other baby? Now she feared she would miscarry our son. She felt as if she had let me down. She felt ashamed.

I called her just to hear the excitement in her voice. She answered as joyfully as she could, but I could still hear the pain in her voice. It was too much for her to hide. I begged her to tell me the truth even though it wasn't the way we wanted it to be. She did as the technician did for her. She sent me a picture of Baby A.

A boy! I must have been so loud inside the hospital lobby because everyone turned to look at me. I couldn't be more excited to hear we were having a boy. I just couldn't keep in the excitement.

I said, "Now, tell me about Baby B. Is it a boy, too!"

Nikki paused for a moment and said, "Hold on, I will send you the picture now." She texted it over and when I opened it, it looked different from the first picture she sent. It only said, "Baby B." Though I don't know how to read these things well, I could see this baby wasn't as big as our son in the other picture.

Nikki said, "Baby B didn't make it."

Not understanding what she meant, I asked, "What do you mean?"

She told me the doctor explained baby B had lost its heartbeat. At that moment, I just couldn't wrap my mind around what she said.

My family could see my reaction quickly changed and were just staring at me as they waited for me to get off the phone to share what was happening with them. I absolutely hated Nikki was home alone and I couldn't hold her right now. It broke my heart knowing she was broken, scared, and alone. Though the loss was devastating, not being with her was excruciatingly painful.

Ultrsound

I stayed just one more day at the hospital and returned home to be with Nikki. I couldn't wait to hold her and assure her I was there for her and our family. We had to focus on the baby we had left and make sure we did everything we could to ensure Nikki's and the baby's health.

Nikki picked me up at the airport. We just stood outside the airport holding each other. I could tell Nikki was blaming herself. Though the doctor assured her it was nothing she did, it still weighed heavily on her. I could see the pain in her eyes and the mental struggle she had inside. As we sat there, Nikki confided in me she couldn't bear losing the other baby.

When Nikki fears something bad is going to happen, she does all she can to distance herself from the situation, so it isn't as painful when it happens. In the coming weeks, Nikki's slipped into another depression. She started to detach herself from the baby she was still carrying in fear of losing him, too. Instead of the joy and glow she once had in being pregnant with our child, she grew distant and cold. I did everything I could to lift her mood and her spirits. She would put a fake smile on from time to time, but inside she convinced herself this Baby would die too so why try to fall in love with it.

Even though the doctors kept telling Nikki the baby looks heathy and bigger than expected, she refused to believe them. To her, her body was just a place to keep him growing for now.

Nikki was great at showing the world a "happier" picture, but I knew the truth. All I could do was tell and show her how much she and the baby meant to me. Hope it would be enough to pull her out and her through this.

Nikki continued to work part time during all this to keep her busy and her mind off things as much as she could. I still worked in an aircraft repair shop near Savannah. We worked, saved, and enjoyed our time together as much as possible. We knew our personal time together would soon be over and we would have to share our time with little man.

The baby naming process was the first time in a long time I saw Nikki a little excited again about the baby. I am Irish and she has a mixture of backgrounds with some Indian. The meaning of a name was important to us both. We got a few baby name books, and we googled a few times. We made a list of the names we liked and narrowed them down. As we sat on the couch laughing and joking about some of the names we came across, I looked over at Nikki. I was overwhelmed by her beauty and the "glow" she had back even if it was just for a moment. It was so nice to see the woman I had grown to adore and love immensely smile again.

We would shout the whole name out to see if the name flowed out easily when we would have to holler their name. We narrowed it down to three names and kept them rolling around our minds for a few more weeks until we settled on Liam. Liam means protector in Gallic. It was a good strong Irish name. It was also unique at the time which made it even more appealing to us. Little did we know it would be the most popular name as he grew up, but for us it was perfect.

Meeting My Family

My Mom was now doing well at home. I wanted everyone to meet Nikki before it would be too late for her to travel. We flew out to Arkansas to meet my family. I just knew everyone would love her as much as I did. The visit went smooth, and everyone enjoyed getting to know Nikki. I showed Nikki around the town, we celebrated my sister's birthday, helped my stepdad fix some things around the house, and enjoyed the peace of knowing we all got along and enjoyed each other's company for the time we were there.

"Accept what is,
Let go of what was,
and have faith in what will be."
- Anonymous[8]

[8] Goodreads.com

Chapter 9

Getting Ready for Liam's Arrival

ONCE WE GOT back home, we had a few short months to get everything together for Liam's arrival. It was busy with baby showers, Nikki's nesting projects, classes, doctors, and work. Before I knew it, he would be here, and I didn't feel we were prepared yet. As the days drew closer, my fear of the type of father I would be grew stronger. I knew Nikki wasn't in the right mindset, so I had to get myself together quickly and be what they both needed me to be.

The due date was finally just a few days away! Nikki was miserable in the Georgia heat. She was ready to get this whole process over with. Nikki went into "labor" a few days early. We started counting the contractions and when they got minutes apart, we went to the center.

They checked her and said, "She is almost there, but not quite ready yet. Go home, take these pills, relax, and get some sleep. He will be here soon, and you will need to be rested."

I asked the doctors how we would know, and the nurse said, "It will be different, you'll know…"

We left confused and said, "Okay, we will look for different."

In the middle of the night, I woke up to Nikki screaming into her pillow trying not to wake me.

She said, "I didn't want to wake you if it was another false alarm again, but this is different!"

I called the nurses, and they said yes bring her in. I drove as fast as I could to get her there. Then, I noticed police lights behind me. The cop seemed to take his time getting out of the car, so I rolled my window down in a panic.

The cop finally reached the window and said, "Sir, do you know why I pulled you over? What is all the commotion about?"

I said it as nicely as I could at the time, "My wife is in labor, and I have to get her to the hospital now!"

The cop shinned his light on Nikki as if I had been lying. As soon as he did, she had another contraction. One foot up on the dash, hollering, and holding her belly. I must admit that one had great timing.

The cop panicked, probably thinking he would he be delivering this baby and instructed me to put on my flashers and get her safely to the hospital.

The birthing center is amazing. They allow you to do as your body tells you to do. Nikki went back and forth for hours between the medicine ball and the shower. She had mostly back labor and was miserable.

Finally, after six hours, Nikki couldn't take the pain anymore and asked the nurse if she could have some meds, but she was too far dilated now and couldn't receive any medications.

Nikki sat on the medicine ball rocking back and forth just humming trying to soothe herself. The nurse would quietly come in and check the baby's heartbeat and told me if Nikki either feels the urge to push or feels like she needs to be on all fours for comfort to let her know. My heart was broken for her. She was in so much pain. I just wanted it to be over for her sake. She was a trooper though, as tough as nails.

Well into the morning hours, Nikki wanted to try the shower again, then went down on all fours and stating the pressure was really bad now.

The nurse checked Nikki and said, "Yes, it's time."

She filled the bathtub and woke the midwife on duty.

The nurses gave Nikki and me instructions and said, "Do not allow her to lift up out of the water. If she does and goes back in, she will drown the baby."

They instructed Nikki with every contraction she was to push as long and hard as she can. Stop when it's over or she can't push anymore.

She started to push and push. Then, I started to feel her raise up out of the water, I gently pushed her back down. I could now see his head! When Nikki saw his face, she froze. She wasn't attached to him yet or ready to be his mother.

Nikki stopped pushing. The contractions came and Nikki refused to push. Emotionally and physically drained, Nikki didn't want to continue this process only to see him not take his first breath.

I gave her some water, a bite of an energy bar, kissed her on her forehead and whispered, "You can do this. Doesn't matter what happens from here, we can get through this together."

Nikki let out a sigh and waited for the next contraction. She did it, he was here! The nurse picked him up out of the water and immediately put him on her chest. They started sucking his airways and he began to cry.

What a beautiful sound to our ears. All I could do was hold them from behind and just look at the precious baby she was holding. I couldn't help but feel like I was holding the whole world at that moment. Feeling the totality of love I felt for them at that moment washed over me.

Nikki needed to rest for a moment, so she got into the bed to try to sleep. The nurse and I went to get the measurements and weight for Liam, 9 pounds 7 ounces, 20 inches long! Wow! He looks good and healthy. Thank God! I took Liam back into the room for us to have some skin-to-skin time so I would have the chance to bond with him while Nikki rested.

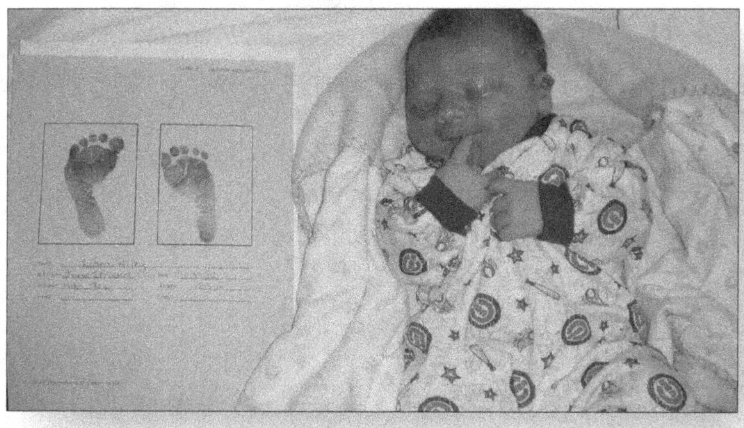

Meet Liam

Never could I imagine loving another as I did Nikki. Nikki had my whole heart already, but now my heart was completely full of all the love I could offer. I knew our family was now complete.

Finally at thirty-four years old, I could say. I have known love and I can love completely.

Proud Papa

In the first few hours, they taught us how to latch Liam for feedings, swaddle him, how to take vitals, and cord cleaning. As we moved Liam around, we noticed he would cry or whimper every time we moved his right arm.

The nurse told us it is common in bigger babies during birth to have their clavicle bone displaced. They instructed us to see a chiropractor the next morning. Just four short hours after Liam was born, we were released and on our way home.

I don't think I have never driven so carefully in my life. I have never driven such a precious cargo before. Then, reality hit me. They are my responsibility to keep safe and secure. I was determined to show Nikki we were a team, and she would never be alone raising our son.

My parents had flown in to help around the house as we adjusted to the parent life. We walked into the house to show off our new bundle of joy to my parents. With him being only four hours old, it did make me nervous for people to handle and hold him. I went straight into protective Dad mode immediately.

Nikki didn't stay with us long. She was exhausted and wanted to sleep while Liam slept. She went into the bedroom, and we stayed in the living room to allow her to rest as long as possible. Unfortunately, it didn't last long before Liam started crying for food. We woke Nikki up, fed Liam, and they both slept a little longer.

I would take him do his vitals, change his diaper, and keep him with me until it would be feeding time. The three of us would lay in bed. I just couldn't help but feel like this is what heaven must feel like. Pure love.

Nikki didn't want to hold Liam very much. She didn't bond with him as I thought she would. She started to feel like she was only there to feed him. It seemed as if all he wanted to do was eat, but we would latch him, and he would just sleep. This became very daunting to Nikki.

Nikki's Postpartum had already started to set in. With the lack of emotional attachment during pregnancy, their relationship seemed to quickly become a love hate between the two of them.

I knew Nikki loved Liam. She didn't want anything to happen to him, but she just couldn't bring herself to want to be with him. When Liam would cry, I would be the only one who could calm him, unless he was feeding.

This made Nikki even more upset. I tried to explain I felt Liam could feel her frustration and anger which didn't help to calm him. She did the best she could to muster up every ounce of love she could to get close to him, but she felt rejected every time she tried. Even though we had been home for a few weeks, their bond still hadn't grown.

The visitors came and left. Everyone was in awe over how precious and adorable he was. Nikki did the best she could to hide the depression, but she never could hide it from me. I was to return to work, yet I feared what would happen with just Nikki and Liam alone. Nikki did the best she could to allow me to get a full night's sleep before my first day back to work.

She stayed in his room all night, feeding, rocking, changing, feeding, rocking, changing. Yet, he screamed through most of the night and slept very little. When I woke up, I found her in his room, and I could see it in her eyes. The fear of being alone with him. The look in her eyes had me afraid of leaving her alone with him.

I called my boss and told him Nikki wasn't ready for me to return, and I had to take off a little longer until I felt safe enough to leave them alone. I stayed home another week with them. Within this week, I did everything I possibly could to take the load off Nikki so all she had to do was bond with Liam.

After three weeks, I thought to myself by now Nikki would be able to work through the postpartum. She could see Liam was alive, doing well, and her fear of him dying would disappear from her mind. Despite all my efforts, though, these two just couldn't seem to bond. I knew Nikki loved him, I knew she was fighting with all she had to beat the depression and fears, but she just kept going backwards.

Liam wasn't the easiest baby. He seemed to never stop crying. We would hold him, feed him, put him down, and he cried. We just couldn't seem to get him calm for long. The doctor would tell us to let him cry it out and we would, but it would be hours. Nothing would soothe him for long. It was taxing on both of us.

I knew I had to stay calm. This postpartum had me nervous. In the tired, weaken, depressive state she was in plus the constant screaming was wearing her down quickly. We would take turns going outside for a walk by ourselves to get away from the crying and try to recenter ourselves.

The week was over, and I had to return to work. Nikki seemed to be ready to take on the days ahead as best as she could. We both thought maybe if it was just them, they would bond a little better and faster.

Unfortunately, we were both wrong. I returned home, took a deep breath, and went inside to see how the day was. My routine was to always give Nikki a kiss, then Liam, and take a shower to "wash work off." Then, I would move into "family mode."

However, my routine went straight out the window. I went inside and Nikki immediately run to the door and handed me Liam. She went outside for her walk as I tried to get Liam to stop crying. When she returned, she stated he had been screaming for hours and nothing she did would work for him. She found herself growing angry when she realized Liam was calm and sitting quietly with me. Nikki stormed into the bedroom. All she could do was cry herself to sleep.

Liam and I sat in the living room as we let Nikki get some sleep hoping when she woke, she would feel a little more refreshed. Feeding time came, she fed him and went back into the bedroom. I gave Liam his bath, made dinner, read Liam a book, cleaned the house, and put Liam to bed. After I got Liam to sleep, Nikki and I needed to try to figure out how to proceed because I had to work again the next morning.

Nikki began to weep stating Liam hated her as much as she hated him. She failed as a mother and a wife. She couldn't get anything done, she wasn't working, and felt like a complete failure. I stopped her from going down her bunny trail.

"Nikki, you are amazing," I told her. "You have fought through all the emotions and pain so far. You will get through this. We will get through this. You and Liam will learn to love each other, just give it time. Things will get better you will see. You are not a failure; you are just feeling defeated right now. You will fight this for your family, and you will come out on top like you always do. You want to know how I know? This time we have each other to keep us pushing forward. I love you and we will get through this."

I just held Nikki and we laid in bed until we both fell asleep.

Nikki and Liam finished the rest of the week together. Some days were more successful than others, but they made it. Liam had an appointment coming up to check on vitals and to see how things were going. We would be sure to talk about how often he cries!

Turns out Nikki wasn't producing enough milk to keep him full, and she wasn't producing enough to feed him enough in a feeding. They suggested we need half and half bread-milk and formula. We did this and it was like we had a new baby on our hands. Yet, it made Nikki's depression worse because now she felt awful for "starving" the baby for six weeks.

Again, she felt it was her fault. I tried to get her to see the bright side. She was now able to let me feed him, and he would be a little happier from time to time.

After weeks of this ongoing cycle, it started to wear me down as well. It was hard to watch Nikki struggle so much. I thought my love would be enough to help her through, but it seemed I could only be there for her. She and Liam would have to do the rest.

We would soon get into a good routine. Liam was calm for longer periods once we got his formula right. Even though Nikki still had a hard time "loving" Liam, she did her best to overcome this depression as well as be the loving wife and mother she could be. We spent the next six months learning to be parents as well as learning our new roles around the house. Even though we had some mountains we were overcoming, we were still so in love, and we loved we had found each other.

Papa and Liam

WE KNEW LIFE WOULD GET BETTER.
IT JUST TAKES WORK AND A LOT OF IT.

"It is not a lack of love, but a lack of friendship that makes unhappy marriages."
- Friedrich Nietzsch[9]

---

9 Goodreads.com

Chapter 10

LIFE'S CHALLENGES

THE WEDDING

NIKKI AND I had talked about marriage often, but we wanted to make sure we were getting married for all the right reasons instead of just because we had a child together. We knew without a shadow of doubt we were meant for each other, so we wanted to move forward and make things right and get married. We didn't have much money, so we decided to elope.

Nikki wanted to have something small, but she was afraid if we eloped, she would never have her "special" day. I looked her in the eye and promised her she would get to have her moment. We set the date for the "day" to be celebrated as October 2, 2009. That would be the day she would get to wear the dress, exchange vows, and have the toast. She went to planning this event quickly because it was only a month away.

We met with my co-worker, an ordained minister, at a local restaurant. We signed the papers, and we were legally married right then and there.

The minister wanted us to be sure we knew it was binding and legal. We went out of the restaurant, said our vows, and I do. Even though it wasn't in a ceremonial setting, it was the perfect day for us. It also happened to be my birthday. She was my perfect gift. I couldn't have asked for a better woman to spend my life with.

We never told anyone we were married already. We just moved forward with planning the "elopement" day for Oct 2. She found a photographer, videographer, small cake, champagne, and a hotel down on Tybee Island. We were to exchange vows on the beach close to sunset. She did such a beautiful job pulling things together quickly. Nikki's talent is saving money while still making events fun and beautiful.

Papa, Liam and Mommy

I honestly didn't care about the dress, or who was or wasn't there. I was just happy to give her the moment she deserved to feel beautiful and have the memories of her special day. She deserved the world and since I couldn't give her the world, I would give her this special day to remember.

THE WEDDING CEREMONY

October 2 finally arrived. She was beaming in excitement for me to see everything she was able to get on the $500 budget! We arrived at the hotel to get ready. Her friend joined us to help get her ready and hold Liam during the ceremony.

Nikki called upon her beauty school friends to help with her hair and makeup. She already looked stunning; I couldn't wait to see the dress. I went to put on my outfit while she got into her dress. When they said I could come out, all I could do was stare at her. How did I get to be the luckiest man on earth and to have her and our son complete my life so perfectly?

We took a few pictures then headed down to the beach. It was a beautiful day. The weather was low 70s with a perfect ocean breeze. The photographer had surprised her by making a heart in the sand with rose petals outlining the heart. There was a small table to the side with our cake and champagne. It was quiet, private, intimate, beautiful, and perfect.

The videographer told me to stand inside the heart, the minister right outside the heart and Nikki to walk up to join me inside the heart. Her friend was to walk out first carrying Liam. They would stand just the left of the heart behind where Nikki would be.

Even though I had seen Nikki earlier, once she came around the corner, she took my breath away again. I couldn't take my eyes off her. All I could think of again was how lucky I was she chose me. The love I never knew was possible was standing there looking me in the eyes and holding my hand.

I never imagined I would be so lucky. I was determined to show them both how much I loved them every day and to be the father Liam needed and deserved. I would work daily on myself to be the best I could for them.

All my thoughts came to an abrupt holt when I heard a phone ringing. She was in the middle of her vows and the minister's phone began to ring. He went to stop the ring and said it was work.

Wedding at the Beach

Wedding Celebration

We all just laughed it off. The minister was so embarrassed. We pulled ourselves together to finish our vows and exchange rings. The best part was I could experience it twice, "You may kiss your bride." We shared the kiss, the cake, champagne, and the pictures along the beach.

We had the most beautiful sunset to enjoy together.

Her friend took Liam back to the hotel so we could have a few quiet moments together. We walked and talked along the beach on the way back to the hotel. We sat on the swing for a few moments holding each other as we enjoyed the sunset, the moment, the silence, and the peace we both had. The day was a success.

Living the married life was amazing. My life was at the highest point I could ever have imagined. We didn't have much, but we had love, respect, loyalty, understanding, and no judgment with each other.

The Job Challenge

Our marital bliss was soon challenged. I found out my job location was closing in the next few months. I would lose my job soon. When I got home, Nikki could tell the day must have been hard for me.

It wasn't the job loss making me nervous. I'd lost everything many times before, but I didn't have a family to feed. If I couldn't provide, what good am I for them?

Nikki is as close to perfect as one could get. She didn't nag. She always listened to the whole story before jumping to conclusions and allowed me to work out what I need to out loud and chime in at the right time. Talking to her was always easy. It was my nervousness I needed to overcome to find the answer.

When I sat down at the table to eat, Nikki asked about my day. I told her about the shop closing and I wasn't sure what we are going to do.

She listened to my fears and then she chimed in, "You didn't like that job anyway."

Immediately, my mood lightened. She wasn't anxious or nervous. She shrugged and said, "Well, it's a good thing we both know how to live having very little. We will be fine. I can work almost anywhere. We will follow you wherever you find a job you really want. I am not married to Georgia. I am married to you."

Even though she helped alleviate some of my anxieties, I was still the man of the house. I had to figure out how I was going to provide for them. I called my best friend to talk things out. He told me he was now working in Afghanistan as a contractor and would love to have me on his team.

Afghanistan? How could I leave my family? Liam was just six months old. Nikki and Liam have a system, but they still don't have a great bond. Could they make it together without me as the buffer and relief? We just got married, how could I leave such an amazing woman and the life we have created?

I thought about what my friend said all the next day. Could this work? Is it the right thing for my family? How could I not wake up with my family every day?

After I thought about it for the whole day, I wanted to bring it up to Nikki and see what she thought. As we sat down to dinner, I told her I spoke with Ralph.

I explained he was overseas and doing well.

I eased the conversation into, "What do you think about me joining him overseas?"

Obviously concerned, she asked, "Are you considering going?"

I explained to her all the pros and cons about it.

After weighing all options both good and the bad, she hesitantly said, "If you think this is the best decision for our family, then I trust you."

After working herself as a contractor with the military for nine years, she knew what I was getting into. She knew how dangerous this job would be. Neither of us were prepared to live without each other, but we both knew this was a good career choice for me. It could open many doors and provide for our family.

I called Ralph back and asked him what I needed to do to apply. After just one phone call on Monday morning, I was booked and preparing to fly out on Thursday.

We hadn't seen it coming so quickly and not much time to prepare. Next thing I knew, it was Wednesday evening. I held Liam until he was fast asleep. I held Nikki all night. How could I leave them in the morning?

Life With a New Job

Morning came whether we were ready or not. We packed the car, savoring every minute together as a blessing. We enjoyed breakfast together quietly. There was a somber mood in the air.

We soon left for the airport, doing our best to hold ourselves together. We knew it was going to be difficult on us both. I wasn't ready to leave my wife and son, but I knew this would be best for our family in the long run. I would do anything for them even if it meant living and working in a war zone.

When we arrived at the airport, Nikki pulled up to the departure zone to let me out so we could just rip the band aid off. She got Liam out of the car as I gathered my things. We stood there holding each other in a family hug for just a few more minutes. Then, with tears in our eyes, we said goodbye and kissed one last time.

As I walked away, I wanted to turn around, tell her we would find another job, how much I loved her, and hold her one more time. I turned to see them still watching me walk away. I blew them a kiss, let a few tears fall, and walked inside.

Nikki returned to the car and finally let out all the tears she had been holding back. She let out all the fear she been trying to hide from me and her anxiety of being alone with Liam. She just sat there and wept. Then, they went to a local park to take a walk and cry.

I also had to let my tears out. I got my tickets, went through security, and went to a restroom. I told myself over and over I was doing the right thing. This was for my family, and I could do this for them. I pulled myself together and went to sit at the gate. All I could do was look at pictures to keep pushing me through the whole reason I was doing this.

My first flight was to California. I would be there one week before heading out to Afghanistan. The week was such a blur. There was paperwork, testing, shots, and training. On my last day there, I decided to take advantage of the local area and do some sightseeing. I went to a local restaurant to grab breakfast. I looked through Google for things to do in the area and the zoo seemed like a great option.

This zoo had many great exhibits with animals you don't see in many zoos. Though it was nice to have a day to myself after all the craziness of the week, the only thing I could think of was how much Nikki would enjoy being here.

I finally got to call home and tell Nikki about my week. She was so excited to hear from me. It was so nice to hear her voice. She hung up and immediately FaceTimed me so she could see my "handsome face." It was so good to see them!

It seemed as if Liam had grown so much already! I could see stress on Nikki's face though she was doing her best to put on a happy face for me. It seemed as if we talked until bedtime like we did when we dated. I know life has led us to this moment apart, but I wanted her to know without a shadow of a doubt how much she meant to me. I let her know I was to leave in the morning. I wasn't sure when I would be able to call again. I wanted to remind Nikki she was doing a great job and if she has a rough day to look at how far they/she/we have come. The two of them were what kept me going.

We'd had to build the ladder of our relationship piece-by-piece, step-by-step. We didn't have anyone to give us a ladder and show us how to step up in life. We may have been behind everyone else, but we knew what we had we earned and worked hard for. We had worked building a life we were now proud of and could get us to who we wanted to be.

I reminded her of how she strong she was, and she reminded me of how much she respected, honored, and loved me. She once again assured me things would be taken care of at home and she would impatiently await my return. She tried so hard to never add more stress to me. I am so grateful for my family.

I was as ready as I could ever be to go. We arrived at the airport and endured the joy of customs. I couldn't wait to get on the plane to start my journey. Plus, it would get me one step and one day closer to returning to my beautiful family.

My tour was to be 90-day rotations with 30 days home. I arrived in Dubai for my overnight stay. The hotel was immaculate, and the service was above par. The food was great, and the beer was, too. I enjoyed going out and seeing the city for the first time. Lots of beauty and wonder in this city.

I enjoyed taking photos of the surrounding areas as well as of the hotel room. It had been a long day, though, so I was ready to head to bed. I needed to prepare my mind for the journey awaiting me the next morning.

I arrived at the airport for my short flight to Kandahar, Afghanistan. The base was one of the largest I had ever seen. It seemed as if once we arrived, it took another hour to get to where I would be staying. I knew the accommodation would be small and underwhelming, but I wasn't prepared for just how small and underwhelming.

We came to some tents at the back of the base, then the driver said, "Home sweet home."

We walked into the tent. It had wooden dividers with a door to each section. It was literally a broom closet with a bed and a small dresser for each person, nothing more.

The restrooms and showers were located a short golf cart ride away in a mobile home looking building called a Cadillac. It was run by non-portable water tanks that were refilled daily. The poo went into what was referred to as "poo-pond." It was pumped into a truck and taken off site. The smell was one we would never forget.

Us newcomers unpacked and began to settle in. They soon had us load up to head over for chow. The food wasn't as bad as I expected.

Afterwards, it was interesting going through the post seeing all the food and shopping options. It was like a mini mart with haggler lines up and down the Boardwalk. It gave post workers something to look for to send home for family as well as meet our needs. It wasn't home, but it was enough for me. I'm a simple man who wanted simple things.

We are 8.5 hours ahead of Georgia time, so calling home would be an obstacle to overcome. I would call before my bedtime which was just as she would wake up, or before she went to bed as I started my day. Sometimes, I would get the opportunity to do both and other days we didn't get to speak at all.

The days we didn't get to speak were always the hardest on both of us. She was dealing with the war inside her mind while trying to take care of our difficult son. I was dealing with the war of getting to know the ins and outs of my new job position with rockets going off all around me. Some were way to close for comfort.

The great thing about this new living arrangement was it forced Nikki and me to talk about literally everything. Decisions big or small, discussions about the future, and what we wanted to get out of this job.

Since communication was key, we had to use some tools to make sure we stayed on the same page. It would be easy for one of us to read a text message or email wrong since we couldn't see the other person's reactions. Up to this point, we had only had one disagreement about a silly washer, and we wanted to keep it that way.

If one of us got upset about something we read or thought we heard the other one say, we would say things like, "What I heard you SAY was... This is how I took it... Is that how you meant it? This is how that comment made me feel..." We didn't have to go through those steps often, but it sure did help us out when we did need them. Even though we were apart, our marriage seemed to continue to get better and better.

The first rotation seemed as if it was never going to end. The 90 days just seemed to drag by. Getting home to hold my wife and son was all I could ever think of. They were all I talked about, dreamed of, worked daily for, and survived for.

My first vacation home finally arrived. I would get to see my family and hold them again in just a few days. I traveled back to Dubai for my layover flight. I went to the same hotel for a hot shower, have a cold beer, a good dinner, and sleep in a comfortable bed.

I was so excited to see my family I could hardly sleep. I looked over the pictures she sent over the past few months. I tried mentally preparing myself to switch back into father and husband mode. The plane ride home was exhausting, but I was so overwhelmed with excitement I didn't even care how tired I was.

They met me outside the airport. Once we locked eyes, we ran to each. We hugged and kissed for a while. I picked Liam up out of his stroller and was taken back by how much he has grown. As we walked back to the car, we had to stop many times for one more kiss, one more hug, and once more glance at each other.

For thirty days, we had each other's undivided attention. Of course, I had a honey-do list a mile long to start working on, but it would wait. First, it was about holding hands, hugging, catching a smile, and listening to Liam's giggling when I tickled him. It was about all the small things we missed that matter the most while I was away.

We agreed not to think about when I must leave again and focus on making memories while I was home. We enjoyed many date nights together by the fire outside after Liam went to sleep. She enjoyed having help again around the house while I enjoyed just being about to touch them and look at them when I wanted to.

I could tell things between Nikki and Liam hadn't changed much in the past few months. Hopefully, she could get a small break with me home. One of the first things Nikki wanted to do was take a nice quiet walk around the neighborhood. I was happy to stay back and spend a few minutes alone with Liam.

Since we only had 30 days to spend together, we decided each RNR home we would take at least one week to travel somewhere to be alone with no distractions, just us.

For our first trip, we decided to go to back to Arkansas to purchase a fifth-wheel camper from my parents. We both enjoyed traveling so we thought this would be a great way for us to see many new places. As we traveled back with the camper, we stopped at a Yogi Bear campground. It was such a great experience. Our first family vacation was a huge success.

Yogi Bear Campground

When we return home, I got a few items on the honey-do list completed. The time seemed to have just flown by. It became time to stay home for a few days to relax as well as prepare for me to leave.

You can never really prepare yourself to leave your family behind and I knew what I was headed back to. Nikki and I sat outside by the fire to talk about what we wanted out of this job. We agreed the priority was to pay down the massive amount of debt we were both in.

Secondly, I was to stay no longer than when Liam started school. However, we both agreed if this job started tearing us apart, I would end it immediately. We both knew it was going to be a huge sacrifice for us all. We just hoped in the end we could say it was worth the sacrifice.

It was time to leave again. I spent the entire morning playing and hugging on Liam. We packed the car and headed to the airport. This time I asked Nikki to leave Liam in the car as we hugged because it was just too heart wrenching to say goodbye again. We kissed goodbye and off I went just as before.

"The purpose of life is not to be happy.
It is to be useful, to be honorable, to be compassionate,
to have it make some difference that you have lived
and lived it well."
-Ralph Waldo Emerson[10]

"You were put on this earth to achieve your greatest self,
to live out your purpose, and to do it courageously."
– Steve Maraboli[11]

[10] Goodreads.com

[11] Goodreads.com

Chapter 11

Things Start Coming Together

Nikki and Liam's Struggles

NIKKI RETURNED TO our empty home to continue her daily routines with Liam. Liam is a very structured child. They had a strict routine and if it wavered even a little, it was sure to be a rough day. Liam was an extremely loud screamer. His cries were never soft even from birth. Liam wasn't the easiest child to raise especially by herself.

Nikki and Liam's relationship was still difficult to describe. Nikki did everything she could to teach Liam all the skills he needed to grow and learn. She played for hours with him. She read to him. She was with him every waking moment.

Though Liam had many great moments, he was mostly a terror for her to deal with. He screamed for hours and hours on end. He would rock back and forth banging his head on the floor or the wall. If she touched him, it made it worse. She would ask the doctors what to do because he would bang his head until he would bleed. They told her to put him in a safe spot and he would eventually stop.

They would go out in public and within minutes he would start screaming uncontrollably. People would stare at Nikki as she would shop. They would pass by her and say things like, "If that was my child, I would whoop his behind," or "I can't believe she is just allowing him to scream like that and do nothing."

What they didn't realize was spanking him only caused the situation to worsen. The only time Liam seemed to be quiet for any length of time was if he was left completely alone in the dark. I called home one day to check on them and Nikki was having a very tough day. After returning home from the store, she put Liam in his darkened room to nap and both then decompressed from their outing.

She told me all about their trip to the store. Nikki was so distraught because this kept happening. She tried Mommy and Liam outings, play dates, shopping, playgrounds. Finally, she was at the end of her rope. She vowed she wasn't going out in public until I was home, or we could get him under control.

I hated I wasn't there or be able to do something for them. I hated she wasn't getting any answers from the doctors on why he screamed so often and so long. I hated this situation for them both. I told her I would be happy to find another job and come home. Nikki said no, we would figure this out somehow.

I begged Nikki to put Liam into a daycare part time, so she could have some time to herself to shop, clean, and take time for herself. She refused because she said he was her job as a stay-at-home mom. The thought of it made her feel like a complete failure.

One day, Nikki was driving home from another awful store trip. She just couldn't take it anymore. She gave into my request. The next day she enrolled him into a daycare center part time; just a few hours three days a week.

By this point, Nikki had shut herself off from the world. Having a child who screamed and had a tantrum so often for no reason caused her to not even want to try to have friends. She felt judged all the time. No one seemed to understand how hard it was for them including me.

The teachers had a hard time with Liam. His screaming disrupted the class. He wasn't quiet by any means. Nikki had warned them about his tantrums and how he had to have a strict routine. Nikki finally felt validated, but worried he would get kicked out of the daycare. They worked with Liam hard for the next few weeks.

Thankfully, he did adjust, for the most part.

Nikki was finally able to have some quiet shopping trips. She cleaned the house with joyful silence. She dared to even join a gym to start working on her weight loss again. She didn't get out often, but I was just so thankful she finally could.

The Jewelry Lady

It had been a while since Nikki went out with any friends and someone from beauty school called her to invite her over to a jewelry party. Nikki didn't want to go because she knew it would be a hassle with Liam, but I convinced her to go.

They arrived at the party. Had some snacks and mingled for just a few moments before the show. Nikki did her best to keep Liam quiet and from being a distraction to the lady doing the show and those watching. Unfortunately, it didn't take long before Liam was into the jewelry lady's bag. Nikki was so embarrassed. She knew spanking him would throw him into hours and hours of tantrums which she didn't want to happen with all these ladies watching.

The jewelry lady just kept on presenting the jewelry and said Liam would be fine. After she finished her presentation, while everyone was shopping through her items she came over to Nikki.

The lady said, "I don't know you, but you need me. It's written all over your face you are mommy all the time and it shows. Meet me tomorrow at 11 a.m. for coffee."

Nikki agreed. After all, she knew she needed something. The next morning, Nikki took Liam to the daycare and met the lady at the local coffee shop. This lady went on to tell her how selling jewelry had changed her life. Nikki wasn't interested.

Then, the lady said, "If I never sell another piece of jewelry again, I'm okay with that. To me the friendships are what keeps me going."

Nikki wanted and needed what this lady had discovered.

My tour was almost up. Nikki had said when I return, she would like me to listen to what this lady had to say and tell her if I think it would be a good idea. So, she scheduled the meeting. The lady went through everything she had shared with Nikki including the cost of startup, how it worked, and so on.

Nikki didn't wear much jewelry. She didn't have any friends or know many people. I didn't know where this would lead her, but I believed in Nikki. I just wanted her happy. I wanted her to have something for her. My investment was completely in my wife. Nothing more. I wanted to see Nikki as proud of herself as I was and have something just for her separate from dealing with Liam and me.

Nikki was the one who wasn't sure enough in herself, but she signed up anyway. I knew how much she doubted herself, so I wrote Nikki a note about how I felt about her taking on this new role as a jewelry lady.

We then enjoyed my thirty days home together. We went on a short trip to Hilton Head Island in the fifth wheel. We just enjoyed being with each other again.

The biggest blessing about this job was it's like coming home to have a honeymoon every ninety days. It definitely gave us both something to look forward to while we were apart.

Things Start to Come Together

I had been overseas for almost a year. The next RNR home, we were to have Liam's first birthday party. During the last ninety days I had been gone, Nikki had worked hard to start her jewelry business as well as on improving her mental and physical appearance.

I had worked hard to overcome my fears of what kind of father I would be shifting back into family-man mode after being in war-zone mode. It was not easy changing from the "bad guy" at work while having rockets landing close by more often than I would like. Don't get me wrong, what I did there was very important for the safety of the missions, but it caused a lot of wear and tear on my mental and physical state.

The only thing getting me through was my family and knowing we were building a better life for our son. I knew Nikki and I had the best relationship we could ever have imagined as we worked to build our family unit together. We had a love worth living and fighting for.

Liam's first birthday celebration was a huge success. My parents and sister were able to come and join in the celebration. Friends and some of Nikki's old coworkers joined in as well. Nikki did an amazing job putting everything together.

My job was to cook the low country boil. I must say it turned out fantastic. As I look back on this visit home, I can't help but feel proud. It was overwhelming as we started to see the pieces of the ladder we had been struggling to find pieces for, finally start to fit and make it look like a "ladder." We were now finding stable pieces to build some sturdy steps on our strong relationship foundation.

My entire life I have waited to find my place and my worth. I sought to find out what love was and learn how to love. I can say finding my soul mate in Nikki and being a father to Liam have given me purpose and given me the love I was seeking. I found my "why" in this life in my family's arms.

Liam's First Birthday

The totality of the purpose of being loved and loving isn't lost on me anymore. My hardened heart is softening slowly. I can't say I have let go of my past, but now all I focus on is my future.

My family deserves to receive the best version of me I can give them. It's a daily choice to wake up and fight through my thoughts to be a better person each day. I desire to give my best in all I do and to be the person deserving of the love Nikki is willing to share with me. My goal is to be proud of the person I am to those around me and of the person I am becoming. Integrity, honor, respect, and loyalty are the values I pride myself on.

As I got ready to return to Afghanistan, I was saddened it was already time to leave again, but I was so grateful I have a family to provide and work hard for as I create a good life for the ones I love.

Looking forward to the trips home for my thirty-day RNR was what kept me going. Often, I wouldn't even have returned to work before we started planning what we would do when I returned home. We both would plan and then compare notes before we settled on our agenda.

THIRTY-DAY RNRs

Over the next few years, we had the opportunity to go to places we had never imagined we would ever get to visit. This job opened possibilities for us to create many wonderful memories. We went on our first cruise which led to many more cruises. We found out we enjoyed exploring new places and being out of reach to the world. We sailed to Jamaica, Mexico, and the Bahamas a few times, and the private island of each cruise line.

Each trip had their own amazing memories. I remember the first cruise we took we swam with the dolphins. It was such a great joy watching Nikki turn into a five-year-old giggling little girl. It warmed my heart knowing I could provide memories for her she and I had dreamed about our whole lives.

Another great memory was when we sailed with another great couple and got to go four wheeling in Jamaica. I, of course goofed off as usual, and slung mud all over Nikki and our friends as we raced along the muddy Touraine. We finished this excursion by jumping off the cliff into the water to clean ourselves off.

When we took our first Disney cruise, I thought I would have some fun and embarrass Nikki to get some giggles. As we entered the ship, they asked our last name. I thought it would be so funny to say "cracker." On the loudspeaker they said, "Welcome the Cracker family." I walked in waving like a celebrity and Nikki entered pushing Liam's stroller with the reddest cheeks and a small side smile. She was always great about allowing me to have my fun.

Shortly after entering the boat, we saw Mickey. Liam just couldn't wait a second longer when it was his turn to meet him. Liam took a running start and when he reached Mickey, he went in for a hug full force knocking Mickey to the ground. As we waited for Liam to get in trouble, Mickey waved off the attendant and wrestled with Liam on the ground for a moment. We helped Mickey up, apologized, and got the picture we had waited in line for. If only Mickey knew how much that moment meant to our family. It's the small moments in life like this we must not forget and be grateful for the experience.

Our First Disney Cruise

I'm grateful Nikki made us dress up for each Captain's dinner. She was just so captivating every time. The pictures to me now are priceless. Our relationship is all about give and take. For me to dress up in a monkey suit was a lot of give I tell you. I am a simple cargo shorts and T-shirt kind of guy.

Although our vacation memories are what kept me going, seeing the growth in Nikki and myself has made me proud. We never accepted being just "good enough" for each other. We never accepted we couldn't do more together. We never accepted the lies we couldn't make this work. We worked hard to attain who we were working toward becoming daily and for what we wanted to achieve as a family.

Over the years, Nikki has overcome her postpartum depression. She soared personally as a "jewelry lady" because it gave her purpose again. She finally fell in love with Liam. Their bond has now become unbreakable. Let me tell you, I truly believe Baby Signing times saved Liam's life and the jewelry saved Nikki's. Sign language helped to calm Liam's tantrums. The jewelry gave Nikki an outlet to focus on just for her, not to mention the friendships she gained from it to say I am proud of her is an understatement. She continues to fight to earn my love every day, as much as I fight to earn hers daily.

**"If one advances confidently in the direction of his dreams,
endeavors to live the life which he has imagined,
he will meet with a success unexpected in common hours."
- Henry David Thoreau[12]**

[12] Goodreads.com

Chapter 12

Our Lives Change Again

I KNOW I didn't talk too much about my life in Afghanistan because it was just mundane and the same almost every day. We did cut loose and have a great time from time-to-time. Rocket attacks became "normal" and the mission stayed the same. Our mission was to keep the pilot and his crew safe as well as the plane in the air. I was not the most well-liked guy there because I wouldn't allow just anything to fly. The plane had to be safe enough I would feel comfortable putting my wife and son on it. If it wasn't, I would not put a pilot and his crew on it either.

The closet I lived in seemed to get smaller every day. My whole world was in the states, I just existed while in Afghanistan and counted the days until I could see my family again. One day, I was missing home and wishing I was with my family again.

One of my coworkers told me,
"If you do for two years what others would never do,
then you would be in a place they would never be."

I took his words to heart. I was willing to put in the work to get my family to a better place. After working there for almost three years, the end was in sight. Liam's school years would be starting which was the end we'd agreed upon.

My next trip home, we took a vacation to Disney World for the first time. If we could do it over, we wouldn't have gone until Liam was a little older, but we still made the most of it. It was short because my honey-do list at the house had gotten quite long. I needed to focus on a getting these things finished up before I left again.

As the RNR was winding down quickly, Nikki and I planned a date night down in Savannah. We enjoyed some much-needed couple time. Finally, I had my long-awaited time with her all to myself. We went to a nice restaurant on the river then walked along the river street enjoying some of the sights we had gone to on our second date. We spent time remembering our beginning, talking about our present, where we want to go for our future, and what kind of job opportunities there would be for me. We discussed her returning to work and where she might be able to go. As we talked about her job, she talked about how frustrated she had been about the people she worked for before. Never having a "good" environment or experience in the places she worked in the barbering industry; she wasn't sure she wanted to return to it.

Cutting Cave

All at once, Nikki threw up hands up and said, "You know what? We should open our own barbershop and call it Cutting Cave. We can create our own amazing place to work."

I jumped up in excitement knowing she was onto something. We began immediately working on a new plan and our new journey began. I was fired up and ready to get this plan started. Once she knew I was 100 percent sold on the idea, the real hard part started for her. She needed to believe in herself enough to follow through. As I returned to work, Nikki started on the business plan and putting in the leg work needed to put our plans in motion.

Once we set the plans in motion, it felt like we would be able to make our plans a reality. However, this meant I would have to be here a few more years than we had planned. I wasn't excited about being here longer, but I was excited to have a business we could call our own. It would be something to be proud of, something to provide for us after this job was gone, and somewhere Nikki would be able to give women a safe place to work. A place to grow their skills, faith, and finances. We would be able to provide a working environment we could be proud of. Even if we failed, we were brave enough to try.

I believed in Nikki completely. She was the hardest working woman I had ever met. I knew she would give it everything she could. I had no reservations in investing in her plan. We were ready to tackle the challenges together.

Nikki went full steam ahead, building business plans, data, stats, and so much more. She took this as her opportunity to build something which would one day be able to support our family as I had been doing the past few years. Every conversation for the next nine months seemed to be only about the business or Liam. Her life revolved around those two It was so exciting to come home and see everything in person she had spoken about via phone or email.

We had been working on the business plan for a year, so the next rotation home we were ready to start looking at locations. Even though Nikki felt like she needed more time, I felt if the right place came along, we were going to take it. We spent my entire thirty days home looking at locations, negotiating leases, and talking pros and cons. I must admit it was exhausting. Locations were being sold right out from under us. The terms of some of these places where crazy to hear!

As my thirty days home were just about over, we passed a shopping center we had passed a million times. I saw a for rent sign in the window. I told Nikki this was the perfect location. We called and set a meeting for the next morning. It used as a nail salon. The plumbing was in place which was the best part about this location. It needed a lot of work and a lot of updating to turn it into a barbershop, but in my heart, I knew this was the place. Even though Nikki was hesitant to move forward because I was leaving again soon, I signed the lease for five years. We were ready. Nikki just needed the push.

When we got back in the truck, we just sat there in disbelief. This was now a reality. We had worked so hard to get ourselves out of debit these past years I had been away. Now, we just got ourselves in the most debt we had ever been in. Crazy as it was, I knew we could make this work. Nikki was ready to put all her efforts into making it work. It was time.

After we signed the lease, I returned to Afghanistan while Nikki and her church family got right to work on the repairs and clearing out the building. The location needed a lot of updating per local code inspection. We called an electrician to come and redo all the wiring plus add in all the outlets needed for the stations. Nikki worked day and night for months trying to bring this dream together.

After working endlessly with her church family, all the while trying to keep up with a four-year-old, Nikki became overwhelmed by the never-ending task before her. She finally gave in and called a handy man to come in and do the rest of the prep work. She was ambitious to take on so much to save money, but her time and sanity were worth the cost of the handyman. In no time, the shop was up to code, put together, and ready for the soft opening.

We faced some hard times, but I could see the positive changes. I did my best to inspect all the completed work. After all, I do it for a living. Nikki was just about to bust at the seams in excitement to open. She set the opening date for January 8, 2014. She met the deadline by the skin of her teeth. I tried to convince her to have a grand opening, but she refused until I got home and could be with her during the big event.

The night before opening, she invited the entire church as well as the opening crew members she had hired to come to her business dedication. It was unusual to have this kind of dedication, but Nikki wouldn't open until she had testified publicly, she would use her business for God's glory and to serve Him through this opportunity He had given us. Even though I am not a "religious" man, it meant a lot to Nikki, and I backed her up 100 percent. The business was prayed over and ready to open.

The next morning the doors were opened, and the real fun began. Getting people in the doors to cut their hair! Although I knew this would take time, I was anxious to build quickly. The quicker the shop could pay for itself the quicker I could come home. It was a slow build, but it meant it was done right. Anyone can be an overnight fad. For us though, we wanted to do everything right, by the book and grow slowly so we didn't get in over our heads.

Liam had started preschool back in the fall so Nikki had a small reprieve to get things done during the day while he was at school. Nikki and Liam got into a now routine with Nikki's new work schedule. Nikki meal prepped and cooked Sundays to get them through the week. She would pick Liam up after school and then return to work until closing. Liam enjoyed going to the shop and helping sweep the floors and playing with the kids who came in. He was so proud of what he could do to be mommy's big helper.

The shop had been open for almost two and half months when my time to come home arrived. I was excited to get home and see it for myself. When Nikki and Liam met me at the airport, they were excited to see me, but even more eager to take me to see the shop. When we pulled up to the shop, it was overwhelming to see the sign up and the finished product. Wow, this was ours! This was what we worked so hard to achieve. Reality set in fast and hard. Liam got out of the car jumping around and so excited.

We walked in and man, was I blown away by how amazing the place looked. The face time and pictures just didn't do this place justice. Nikki worked so hard, and man, did it pay off. Liam wanted to give me the grand tour. He wanted to start in the back because it was his area where he got to "play" in mommy's office. Liam took my hand and off we went.

"Papa, here is mommy's office, the bathroom, the wall of bacon, the handprints wall the kids get to do after their haircut, and my favorite part, the toy box!"

He was so precious and excited. I was so unbelievably proud of them both and seeing all their hard work come together.

This tour home would be the beginning of my second job as Nikki's maintenance man. I was okay with that because one day she will be my "sugar momma" and this was the starting point. My thirty days went by too quickly. Between the house honey-do list and now the shop's list I was very busy. It was worth it, though because my family is worth it. I got everything finished on the list and we got to sneak in a few moments alone in the evening after her shift was through.

The best part of this trip was being able to help take the load of Nikki, even if it was only for a short time. Cooking is a passion of mine and man-oh-man did they enjoy having a fresh home cooked meal daily. Cooking, cleaning, taking care of Liam, and getting the checklist done were my greatest achievements this visit.

Sadly, soon it was back to the rat race for both of us. I got back to work safely. Nikki went back into the routine she and Liam had established. Both our lives were so busy. I hated we didn't get to talk daily anymore. If we did get to chat, it would be a quick briefing on how things were going, and I love you. I didn't like what the busyness created. I changed my routine so I could call her more. I would wake up earlier so I could call her when she got off work. I would often stay up late just to hear her voice and to say good morning to her and good night for me.

It put a lot of strain on us both. However, since our relationship was rock solid, I knew we could survive this situation. I couldn't have been more grateful because I knew many of our coworkers and friends who wouldn't have survived a situation like we were in.

I worked hard to keep the shop doors open financially while Nikki worked hard at growing the business. We made a great team. We supported each other. We believed in each other and pushed each other to do better.

We were able to accomplish so much

because we were willing to put in the work

and stand by one other.

The shop numbers grew monthly. The shop had been open almost a year. Even though there wasn't an end in sight for me yet, the numbers were headed the right direction. Although I missed my RNRs just relaxing with my family in the middle of nowhere, I settled for being with them every day and working alongside them. It felt great to come home and work on something ours!

**“What we have once enjoyed we can never lose,
all that we deeply love becomes a part of us.”
– Helen Keller[13]**

[13] Goodreads.com

Chapter 13

LOVE, LIFE, AND LOSS

NIKKI AND I were going to celebrate our fifth wedding anniversary when I came home in October. We had talked about having a reception one day since we couldn't afford one when we got married. Nikki suggested doing it for our fifth wedding anniversary. I completely agreed it was a wonderful idea!

Nikki went full steam ahead on getting the whole day planned for us. Her excitement for the reception had gotten all her team members as well as the church members excited about helping her get the event planned. During the slower times at the shop, the ladies would help Nikki make the centerpieces and table decor. Fall is our favorite season, so naturally Nikki decided to have the decor in all fall colors.

Nikki is the queen of cheap yet beautiful décor. She collected the big cans of food from church after the Wednesday night dinners. Once she had enough matching cans, she cleaned them out, put burlap ribbon around each one and added beautiful fall-colored flowers inside. Then she collected yogurt cups, wrapped twine around them, and used them to hold the trail mix on the tables.

Even though we had only a little money to spend, she enjoyed making the items herself to use the money we had for the bigger stuff. Thankfully, her church family told her they had decided they would all come together and make a dish for the dinner taking a lot of stress off Nikki.

When I tell you Nikki thinks about every little detail, she even created crafts for the kids, and hired someone to watch over them so the kids and parents would have a great time. She hired a local DJ with a great reputation. She had friends who made her cakes and took our family photographs.

Our anniversary was on October 2, but we would celebrate a little later in the month to align the celebration with my RNR time. It doesn't matter to me what I am doing while home as long it is with my family. However, I was definitely looking forward to finally giving Nikki the reception she had been waiting for and deserved. It was an evening to share our love and joy with our family.

I couldn't wait to see everything Nikki had told me about come together. The months seemed to drag by for me, yet fly by for Nikki. It's amazing how we have lived apart for almost four and a half years, yet we are getting stronger every day. I am so blessed to have someone who wants to work as hard as I do to make this work. The communication over these years has been critical to us making this marriage work so well.

The months finally went by, and I was on my way home again. I was excited to be home and celebrate with my family, and to see the growth in the shop. Most of all to see my amazing wife and our growing monkey boy. They truly are my heart and soul.

The shop had grown so much. We now had four amazing stylists. Nikki had gotten the hang of this work and mommy life routine down to a science. Liam and I got a lot of one-on-one time since Nikki was working. I picked up the household and Liam duties again which I always enjoyed. I never thought it was fair to Nikki I always got to be the "fun" parent, but man did I enjoy being it.

I was only home a few days before our reception was to happen. My part was to show up in my wedding outfit and enjoy myself. I did help Nikki finish up a few of the very small details, but she already had everything completed.

Nikki and her friends went early to decorate the location. We decided to have the reception in a small community center close to where Nikki was attending church. It was very accommodating with an outside covered area and a playground. It was also for a great price for the size and central location. The community center had a full kitchen and a main room with a few small classroom- size rooms down a small hall. Nikki used one of these rooms for the kids to enjoy their activities with the sitter while their patients enjoyed the celebration.

In the main room, they had the tables lined up from the entry door to the middle of the room, so we would have some dancing room in the front. Nikki, loves to dance, I love to embarrass her with my dancing, so the room to move on the dance floor was important. Just beyond the dance floor was the kitchen. It was to be lined with the most delicious southern dishes and desserts.

The tables were perfectly decorated with the can centerpieces Nikki had made, along with snack bowls, tea lights, and fall colored flowers. It was perfectly spaced out and beautifully displayed. Off in the right-hand corner, Nikki had a small photo-booth area set up with our camera on the tripod and props. She used a rustic white bench handmade for her with burlap curtains behind the bench. Nikki had our wedding pictures set up on a small round table with our cake. I was also able to get our projector to work so we could play our wedding video.

Everything was set up and it was time for Nikki to get ready. She had chosen not to wear her wedding dress since she had lost so much weight. She is beautiful no matter what she wears. Comfort before beauty was what I always told her. She found this royal blue dress. It had a very small train in the back with a few small rhinestones in the front. When she stepped out of the dressing room, she had such a radiant glow about her. She took my breath away. I could only stare and think to myself again, "How did I get this lucky?" It's not just her outer beauty that stops me in my tracks. It's who she is and the heart of pure gold inside her gorgeous body.

As the guests started to arrive, I took Nikki outside to have a short private moment with just us.

Our Fifth Wedding Anniversary

I took her by the hands, looked her in the eyes and said passionately, "Nikki, you have made me the happiest man these past five years. We have accomplished so much in such a small amount of time. You have given me a son. You have truly given me life. It brings me so much joy to be able to celebrate with you this evening. I wish we could have done this reception five years ago, even though I think it is even more perfect today. I would marry you a hundred times and I will celebrate our love for the rest of my life not just tonight. Before we get distracted with evenings events, I just wanted you to know how beautiful you look and how proud of you I am.

Nikki held back the tears as I spoke. She told me I was the best part of her. I kept her fighting daily to do better and work harder. She told me how much she respected the man I am. She was proud to share my name because it truly was the only thing I had to offer her when she married me. Carrying my name was an honor for her and Liam to have. Everything else we have in life above who we fight to be was just a bonus to her. She said she loved how hard I work daily to earn their love and provide for us.

She then leaned in to just hold onto me for the moment. We shared a beautiful kiss then went back inside to greet our guests. As everyone entered, there was a small smooth tree plank we had everyone who attended sign. We had a small thank you gift which was a small carabiner that read, "Anthony and Nikki hooked since 2008." No detail was missed or left out.

The whole building was soon filled with the greatest aroma of all the southern dishes you could ask for. Once the food was all in place, the pastor said grace. Nikki, Liam, and I lead the line into the kitchen entering from one side and exiting out the other side.

We sat at our designated table up front. As our guests began to sit down to eat, we played the video from our actual wedding day. It was amazing to relive one of our greatest memories with our closest friends and church family. As the video came to an end, the D.J. began to play some music softly in the background as everyone ate.

Once Nikki and I finished our meal, we finally got to have our "first" dance. The theme song for our lives together has been "Right Time" by Warren Barfield. Nikki heard this song at a comedy show she went to, and Warren was the opening act. The song made her cry immediately as it had our life down to "a T." We had listened to this song a million times before now, but at this moment it felt even more special than ever before. As we danced, I held Nikki close and just took in the moment. As we looked out over the crowd, we saw the song had touched them so deeply, most of the guests were crying.

As our dance ended, almost everyone had finished their dinner and now the real fun began. Immediately after our dance, we had the mother and son dance followed by the father and daughter dance. The dance floor was now open for the rest of the evening. I have to say again I have no rhythm at all, but it didn't stop me from joining in and having a blast. Our guests joined Nikki and me on the dance floor, and we danced the rest of the evening away. Everyone had such a great time.

The photo booth was a huge success. We still enjoy looking over all the pictures the guests had taken. We smile every time we think back to all the fun everyone had. To say the night was a huge success would be an understand.

Photo Booth Fun

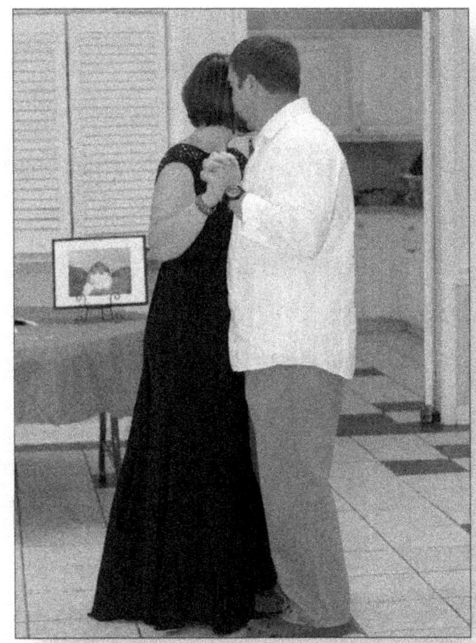

Our First Dance

Mother / Son Dance

I wish Nikki and I could have snuck away to have our long-awaited honeymoon, but that wasn't the case. Work duties came first. The next day was Sunday, so we took the day to go to church and just recover our aching muscles for the week to come. Come Monday, Nikki went back to work, and Liam returned to school. I got some much needed me time to relax at home before I had to head back to work myself. I just sat back on the recliner while listening to the silence of the house around me. I enjoyed just taking it all in. and looking at the walls covered in photos of us over the past five years.

We finally had furniture that matched and a playroom for Liam. There was a nice size kitchen for me to cook in while I was home. Liam had a safe place to lay his head nightly. I have the love of my life supporting me every day. I just couldn't picture my life turning out this amazingly. I sat there a little while longer in awe of the things Nikki and I have been able to accomplish.

I got up to cook dinner with such pride to be able to do this for my family. I took a nice fresh hot home-cooked meal to Nikki at work. Then, I gave her a hug and kiss before I shot out the door to pick Liam up from the bus stop. These are the things people think are mundane, yet these are the things I look forward to the most.

Unfortunately, the day came when I had to head back to work. We dreaded the day every time, but we both have our routines to return to.

Over the next year, our lives were pretty "normal." Work and more work. One of my trips home, I got to join Nikki and her workers on a company outing doing a ghost tour in Savannah. Nikki really enjoyed getting the team together outside of work to help build up the family culture she worked hard to maintain.

They have taken tourist tours downtown and gone to trade shows all over the southern coast. Then there were the epic Halloween and Christmas parties. Nikki really worked hard to be the boss she had always wanted. It has been great watching her come into her calling.

After five years of being overseas, I was burnt out. Nikki seemed to be getting really used to doing everything on her own. I just couldn't stand to watch Liam grow anymore without being home to be with him. Nikki and

I had to have a hard discussion about making the timeline for me to come home permanently.

After some discussion, we decided no matter how the shop was doing or what was going on in our lives, I would come home the following year. This gave us both something to work toward and look forward to. I know no matter what, I would be out of here soon!

Tragedy Hits Hard

It was May of 2015, and I was home on my RNR getting things done around the shop for Nikki. The first Tuesday of every month, Nikki would go to the homeless shelter to cut the men's hair there. While Nikki was there, she received multiple calls from her stepfather in Indiana. In between a couple of guys, Nikki called him back. He said her sister had been shot and killed.

Nikki fell to the ground and wept. The guys all around her were extremely concerned and immediately ran to get the director of the facility. A few of the gentleman escorted her to the office, while other men protected her personal items.

A few started cleaning up the station where she worked in the corner. After a few moments in the office, she pulled herself together enough to tell the director about her sister.

The director and the few men still with her prayed for her and the family immediately. Nikki stayed in the office talking with the director until she was calm enough to drive. The gentleman helped Nikki load up her car. They all gave her a hug and told her they would be praying for her.

Nikki drove to Liam's school to pick him up as she always did on Tuesday. She just sat in the parking lot making phone calls to other family members as she tried to wrap her head around what was happening. She called their father, siblings, and their stepmother. Those were the hardest phone calls she had ever had to make.

Nikki pulled herself together to go inside and pick Liam up from school. The teacher immediately knew something was wrong. Knowing I worked in Afghanistan, she was frightened something had happened to me. Nikki let her know her sister had been killed. She could do nothing but give Nikki a hug and say a prayer for her.

Liam also knew something was wrong. He kept asking mommy to tell him what was wrong, but she just couldn't.

In the car, Nikki told him, "Mommy has to make a few more phone calls and I need you to be very quiet please so I can talk."

Liam agreed to stay quiet as Nikki called a friend from church to start the church prayer list for her family.

By this time, Liam had heard everything and his little five-year-old brain had put everything together and he knew mommy was in pretty bad mental state. As they pulled into the shop, Nikki remained in the car to finish the call as Liam ran inside. He ran straight to me and began to tell me everything he had overheard.

I immediately ran to meet Nikki outside. I could see from her face everything Liam had said was true. I couldn't say anything as Nikki just collapsed in my arms.

She just started screaming, "She's gone, she's gone." I barely kept her standing upright and I just held her to allow her the time to scream and cry. She needed to get it all out before she went inside to the shop. She just couldn't stop crying.

Liam let all the workers know mommy's sister had been shot and was dead. The ladies come out to give Nikki a hug and told her to go home, they would get everything worked out at the shop.

I eventually got Nikki to go home. Her best friend came over and brought a fried chicken dinner for us as Nikki tried to get her flight arrangements made. I was just so thankful I could be home to help her. Nikki flew to Indiana the next day. I stayed home to take care of Liam and the shop so Nikki wouldn't have those concerns while dealing with everything awaiting her.

Once Nikki arrived, she had to hit the ground running. Her family had set up the meeting with funeral home to make the arrangements. Once those where made, they had to meet with investigators at the police station.

Calls had to be made to friends with the funeral details. They had to find something for everyone to wear, and the list just kept going on and on.

Her sister also had two daughters. One was sixteen and one was turning thirteen in just a few days. Nikki couldn't imagine what it must be like for the kids losing their mother because she knew how hard it was for her. Nikki decided to push the service back a few days, so they didn't bury Angie on her daughter's thirteenth birthday.

Nikki decided to take the family out to celebrate her niece's birthday so she could have a small hope of a little happiness on her birthday. They decided to go for a fun trip to drive go-carts, bumper boats, and play arcade putt-putt. They finished off with dinner and cake at home. The fun-filled day did help a little, but everyone knew what was to follow the next day.

The next morning, Nikki went ahead of everyone else to set up the location and ensure Angie looked like the way they remembered her. The family followed a few hours later, though to Nikki it seemed like just minutes had passed. The family arrived for their time before everyone else was allowed in. Of course, it was a somber moment, but it was the first time the family has been together in years.

They all shared great memories and looked through all the photos they had found.

Then, the guests arrived. More people than Nikki would have imagined showed up. Friends from Angie's high school, old boyfriends, cousins Nikki hadn't seen in years, but Angie had kept in contact with. Nikki's friends came to support her, too. Then the family members who only come out of the woodwork for weddings and funerals. Among the crowd were the detectives as well. It was a great turnout Nikki wished would have never been necessary.

The burial was beautiful, but by this point Nikki was so mentally and physically drained, she just knelt and hugged the casket. She wept not wanting them to lower her sister down into the ground forever.

Nikki finally moved back, and the guests began to leave. Nikki remained until the dirt was completely replaced where her sister's casket just sat. Nikki placed a rose on the dirt while taking one rose home with her. Though she was surrounded with love, Nikki was ready to be home with Liam and me.

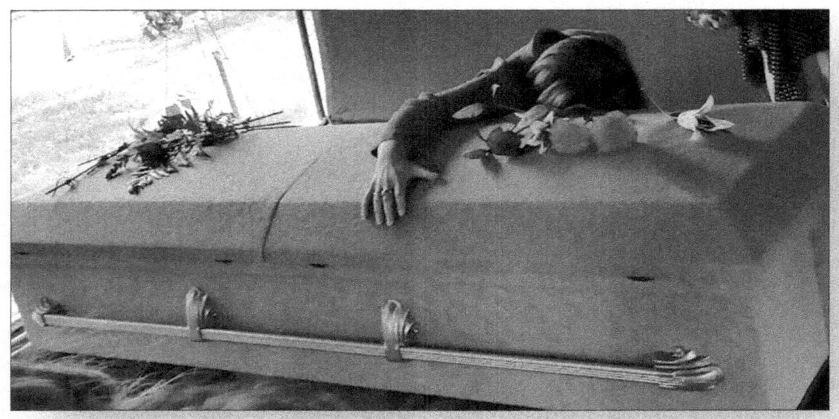

Nikki at Her Sister's Casket

Nikki flew home just a few days later. I just sat on the couch next to her holding her for hours. I hated I couldn't take this pain away from her and her family. Instead, I just sat in silence holding Nikki, allowing her to talk as freely as she wanted though she mainly sat in silence.

The rest of my stay home I did everything I could to support Nikki emotionally. Nikki returned to work, a mess, but was there. She struggled with guilt and blame.

Nikki had begged her sister to move to Georgia. We flew her and her girls down to spend the summers with us many times. Unfortunately, Angie wanted to stay in Indiana. Nikki knew she was in a bad relationship and did what she could, but it just wasn't enough. Nikki fought to let Angie know she was worth more and deserved more. Angie stayed despite her family begging her to leave. Nikki struggled with the guilt and wished she hadn't given up trying to convince her to leave. She thought if she had fought for Angie a little harder maybe she would be alive today.

I hated to leave Nikki in this state of mind. I called my boss and got a short extension to my stay, but I would still have to leave her shortly. Nikki just died inside. She fought daily to smile, but she just couldn't fight the tears for very long. Her friends tried to keep her busy, but Nikki started to refuse their invitations to hang out. Liam tried to make her giggle, though she tried to make Liam feel better, she just couldn't break through. Sadly, Nikki just sank into depression allowing the sadness and guilt to consume her.

I returned to work feeling uneasy about leaving Nikki, but I knew she had pulled herself out of the darkness before. I believed she could do it again. The next few months, Nikki felt like she just couldn't shake this depression. She felt like she couldn't be the wife, mother, and manager she needed to be. She asked the shop manager to watch over things to give her the time to deal with this grief.

One day as Nikki was trying to think of someone who could watch after Liam for a little while, she cried out to God. Immediately, she felt the presence of God with her. He told her Angie was with Him and she was alright. Suddenly, an overwhelming feeling of peace swept over her. Nikki was still extremely troubled and saddened by losing her sister, but God gave her the peace of mind her sister was at rest in His arms.

This gave her the peace she needed to be able to start the healing process. Nikki was able to pull herself out of the depression once again, and be the wife, mother, and boss she needed to be for those who loved her. She was able to process the loss and start to move forward in a healthier manner.

Life always continues to happen to all of us. Sharing life with someone you love is a blessing. Nikki and I counted our blessings daily, especially after the painful loss.

This tragedy reminded us just how precious life is, and how quickly it can be over.

Nikki, Angi, & Their Mother

REST IN PEACE ANGIE 1980-2015

"Families are the compass that guides us. They are the inspiration to reach great heights, and our comfort when we occasionally falter."

- Brad Henry[14]

[14] Goodreads.com

Chapter 14

Home for Good!

NIKKI WAS A networking machine the next few months. She talked to everyone who come into the shop about job openings at the local aircraft manufacturing company. It turns out one of our employees knew some people who oversaw the hiring and could help me get my foot in the door there.

Even though I was six months out from our end date, I started applying for jobs. I applied for job after job, and I got a denial letter time after time. I was getting nervous I would have to start applying for places not around home. If I was going to be in the states, I wanted to be with my family.

One day, I opened yet another denial letter. Feeling defeated, I called Nikki and told her I was going to start applying for a few jobs at other aircraft facilities across the states. It would be a temporary job until I could get one closer to home. She said she thought one would come through near home, but it wouldn't hurt to apply just to be safe. We discussed if I did get a job out of state, I could live in the camper, and come home on my days off if the job was close enough. It was better than our current situation. It still wasn't ideal, but I would be able to see them more often.

I continued my workday not liking my new job options. I was ready to get back to the tent to get some much-needed rest. The day just seemed to drag by. I feared I would end up here longer or not being in Georgia with them. With the shop being open, relocating our family wasn't ideal either.

I got to my room and just fell on the bed in defeat and despair. I hated this feeling. I opened my phone to look through pictures of Nikki and Liam. The pictures always helped me through when I felt depressed. After looking through a few pictures, I get a notification of an email. I change screens to the email. It read, "Congratulations on moving on to the next stage in the hiring process. Your application has been forwarded to the hiring manager. You will receive a call soon to set up an interview."

It was the email I have been waiting for! It was the same job I got the denial email earlier, now they were considering my application. I knew it was extremely early for Nikki, but I just had to tell her. I called her at 3:30 a.m. She answered in a panic thinking something was wrong for me to call so early.

After she said hello, I just busted out in excitement. "Baby, I have an interview coming up! This is what we have been waiting for! If I get this, I will be home with you and Liam! Oh baby, is this really happening? Do we finally get to be together full time? I love you so much and I can't wait to hold you every day and kiss you goodnight every night. I am so ready to be home!"

Nikki didn't say much. She just allowed me to talk and express all my excitement. She mustarded up as much joy as she could after being woken up. She assured me I would nail the interview and in no time we would be together. We talked just a short time because I knew she had a long day of work ahead of her.

It took me a while to fall asleep with so much excitement inside. I finally fell asleep dreaming of how life would be so different for us soon. I know it's a chore to take Liam to school every day, but I was looking forward to it. The small things are what I constantly think of and miss.

The day I received the email from the manager, it included his phone number. The time on the email wouldn't work with my current job location. So, I called the gentleman and let him know I was in Afghanistan and would be happy to do a phone interview at the allotted time if it was an option. He said it would be fine and he would look forward to my call.

The time zones made this a little tricky, but it was worth me staying up late for it. The anxiety of waiting to have the interview would have kept me up all night anyway. I laid in bed just staring into space waiting for the time to pass, and dreaming off the life being home daily. It was finally time to make the call. As the phone rang, it felt as if my heart was going to pump right out of my chest. The pressure I felt to get this job was unreal.

The gentleman answered the phone, and we began to talk about my current position. Most of what I did was classified information, therefore, the answers I gave were vague and short. They were typical interview questions and easy to answer until he got to the availability question.

"I was looking to being home within the next few months if the slot became available," I told him. "I am looking to work the weekend shift when it opens up. I would like to spend the rest of my week making up for lost time with my family."

After we spoke, he said, "Thank you for your time. We will be in touch." That didn't assure me, but I knew a lot of these places had multiple steps in the hiring process. I hung up the phone not knowing what to expect next.

I finally fell asleep. It felt like just minutes later my alarm went going off. I reluctantly got up and went back to my mundane daily routine. It wasn't long into my workday I received an email from the company in the states. They were requesting a second interview. I was blown away. It was working out so quickly. I immediately responded I would be able to do my second phone interview at the same time the next day.

Dare I dream to have my hopes up so high?
Is this really ending my time in Afghanistan this quickly?

I stayed up again with nothing but sheer hope this was going to be the phone interview I had been looking forward to for the last five years. The gentleman I had spoken to the last time answered the phone within just a few rings. He let me know his boss was on the line and had a few additional questions for me.

They said, "Let us cut to the chase. We want to have you join our team. We have heard great things about you, and we will make a spot for you. When are you able to start?"

I was floored. I didn't expect that at all. My mind was racing a million miles a minute. I told them my next trip home was scheduled to be in

October and I would be happy to start them. That would give me just under sixty days' notice at my current job and enough time to start sending my items home. It would give my current employer time to fill my position and give the new job time to find a position for me to walk into as well.

I couldn't stop the excitement from beaming out of me. I called Nikki immediately to give her the great news. I could hear it in her voice she was shocked to hear the news. She was so excited, she started telling everyone at the shop immediately I was coming home!

I couldn't hardly believe it myself. I couldn't just lay there and go back to sleep so I did the only logical thing I could think of, I started packing.

I began filling my footlocker with all the things I had been collecting while here. It included knives I had with the mission info engraved on them, and clothing I had been given by a few of the local workers. I also packed the letters from Nikki from over the years.

I was so eager to get to work. I went straight to tell my boss I would be taking a job state side come my next scheduled RNR. He wasn't surprised to hear the news. I had been honest about how I was looking for something closer to home.

We had become friends over the years, and he knew I was ready to be home. He hated to let me go, but he understood it was time for me to be home with my family.

I took my time from the lunch break to take the footlocker I had packed to the postal service tent set up near the center of post. It was the best feeling in the world. I put the final touches on the outside of the box and paid the shipping fees with a smile. I returned to work thinking it didn't matter what hit me, nothing could bring me down.

Coming Home

It felt like no time at all I was clearing and cleaning out my room. I can't lie, I did enjoy what I did here. Leaving such a great work family was hard to do, but my family needed me, and I needed them.

I shook hands with some amazing men one last time. Hugged some necks and told them to look me up if they were ever in Savannah. I headed over to the postal tent one more time to send off all the rest of my things, so I didn't have too much to carry with me. On my journey to the postal tent, I thought how I won't miss the poo pond or the showers here at all.

After sending everything off, it was time to head to the airport to catch my flight to Dubai. Although I enjoyed most of my visits to Dubai, this visit seemed surreal. Knowing I wouldn't see the hotel ever again, I enjoyed a meal and a Guinness with my buddies who were on their RNR. When I got back to the hotel room, I took a shower then just sat and stared out the window at the beauty the place had to offer. I daydreamed about the life Nikki, Liam, and I would have soon. I drifted off to sleep dreaming of my love's arms around me every night for the rest of my life.

After some much needed sleep, it was time to go to the airport to fly to Atlanta. I never looked forward to going through customs, but just knowing it is the last time for a long, long time if not forever made it easier to look forward to. The flight was a great flight. I couldn't have asked to end this chapter of my life on a better note.

I reached Atlanta and had just a short layover before catching my flight to Savannah. I called Nikki to let her know all my flights were on track, and I would be home on time. Nikki was so excited to welcome me home. I knew it was a workday for her, so I would have to go back to the shop for just a few hours until the end of her shift. I was 100 percent okay with that. Home was with her no matter where or what we were doing.

As I boarded the flight, Nikki went to pick up Liam from school. Liam knew I was coming home, but he didn't know I was coming home forever. Nikki and Liam stayed on routine going back to the shop until about 15 minutes prior to my arrival time. After pacing around the shop for a little while, they headed to the airport.

They pulled up to cell phone lot until I let them know I had landed. Once I landed, they hurried over to the arrival flights section and got set up. I didn't have anything to collect from baggage claim because I sent it all via mail. I didn't want anything else stopping me from getting out of those doors.

I rushed out as quickly as I could and found them standing behind this giant welcome home sign Liam's kindergarten class had made for me. It was such a beautiful sight to see the excitement on his face to see me and how proud he was of their sign. Nikki was standing there beautiful as always. We just had a family hug and kiss. We were so grateful it was the last time we had to have these welcome home moments. I was beyond ready for our next chapter to begin.

Welcome Home Papa

"Family time is not a matter of convenience.
It is a matter of priority."
- Anonymous[15]

[15] Goodreads.com

Chapter 15

LIVING OUR BEST LIFE TOGETHER AGAIN

I STARTED WORK shortly after arriving home. The weekend shift was perfect for me. I was able to be home Monday through Thursday and take care of as much as possible while Nikki worked. Then, I worked thirteen hours Friday through Sunday. It wasn't great for a social life with our friends, but it was what my family needed.

I took over just about everything so Nikki could have a break from having carried this whole load for the last five plus years. At first, she was very reluctant to let everything go, so I took each task away from her slowly.

Cooking was her least favorite and my absolute favorite. I cooked dinners every day. I would spoil Nikki every evening with a fresh hot cooked meal at work. I would even cook extra meals on Thursdays so Nikki would only have to heat up the dinner for Friday and Saturday. Sundays were always leftovers day or cheap quick and easy, so Nikki didn't spend her only day off cooking anymore.

Keeping a balanced meal plan and knowing what to cook wasn't my strong point so Nikki would make the menu every Sunday evening. Then, Monday I would happily go to the store and collect all the groceries needed for the week. We each picked a meal we wanted one night. It almost never failed for Liam to ask for taco night. Cheese dip has been this kids' obsession since he was a toddler.

Once we handled the meals and dinner routine, I started picking Liam up from school and doing his homework with him. Though this task sends most parents into fits and fights, I enjoyed the task. Just spending the time with Liam, working with him, and seeing how smart he was were all things

I hadn't been able to enjoy while I was away. The projects were always fun for us. Liam and I got into a routine quickly.

A few minutes of TV while I heated up dinner. We would eat and enjoy each other's company, talk about our day, and then we would do homework. It was a well-oiled machine. If homework went well, he would watch a little more TV until bath and bed. Nikki would come in around bath time, then put him to bed. They would always be his talk and prayer time.

After getting Liam off to sleep, it would be our time together for just a short one hour before we went to bed as well. On nicer evenings, we would sit outside snuggled up around a fire. We would watch a show or just lay in bed and talk.

I had missed the smell of her hair, the laughter from tickle time with Liam, and play fighting king of the bed with the three of us were some of the little things I missed the most. The family hugs I would force them to stop everything and do before we left the house in the mornings were at the top of the list!

Being home and sharing the family load together is what life is about. Both of us were working hard daily for our family as a team on everything. We did what needed to be done to help the other out. We have seen what we didn't want in our lives growing up. So, we worked hard daily to be a team and still communicate effectively.

Even though we didn't get to go on trips as often, just looking forward to seeing them every night was enough for me. I didn't know just how much Nikki and I would accomplish, but I knew we could do anything together.

Nikki continued to bust her butt at work. With me home she was able to focus more on growing the business and go to more marketing events. I supported her 100 percent and picked up as much as I could so she could focus clearly. She finally saw her hard work payoff when the shop earned an award from the local magazine for readers' choice best hairstylist in 2016. This award came as a surprise to the whole team.

We worked hard to build relationships with our guests, not just turn a chair. It was nice to see our guests felt the same way back. This award will always be special to us. We were able to go to the dinner together and humbly accept the award. We talked to a few other business owners who won as well before we went back to the shop to celebrate with the team.

We knew we were nothing without our amazing team. We spoiled them as often as we could. We successfully created a work environment we were proud of where none of the ladies feared coming to work. It was a place to grow as a team, personally, expertise, and spiritually.

Readers' Choice Best Hairstylist in 2016

Nikki continued to be active in as many church activities as she could. Staying busy with work, family, and friends made it hard to serve outside of work activities. She started a Bible study for her workers, and did outreach community projects as often as she could with her team. If she couldn't be a part of all the church activities, she would faithfully be at the church on Sundays. I have always admired Nikki's faith. I respected her decision to seek God first. It kept her centered and grounded. I was so proud of her.

I bragged on her at work as often as I could. She did the same when she had the chance. Most of the time she didn't have to brag because her team would always remind her what a great guy I was.

The years started to fly by with how busy our life was. Nikki's award-winning shop was growing like crazy with more and more staff and more guests to serve. Awards came in the mail out of the blue. Though we were proud and grateful for each one of them, we kept trying to earn the next haircut in the chair.

We had a lot of date nights at home. Very rarely we would go out to dinner in the evening. We mostly craved out lunch dates while Liam was at school.

Liam's Second Grade School Formal Winter Dance

One evening, Nikki was so excited about Liam's second grade school formal Winter Dance. Dressing up and dancing are two of her favorite things to do. After they arrived, her expectations of dancing the night away with Liam was cut short. Liam ran off with his friends and was seen rarely throughout the rest of the evening. Nikki would join in on the line dances to enjoy herself. Liam came and stopped her since the other parents were not dancing. Nikki found a seat and just sat the rest of the evening.

She texted me and said Liam ditched her and wouldn't let her dance with or without him. I knew how much she had been looking forward to it.

I didn't want the night to be completely ruined for her, so I went home a little early, showered as quickly as I could, and put on my suit from our last cruise.

I lowered the lights, played a Louie Armstrong with Ella Fitzgerald song softly in the background. I stood in the kitchen holding a single rose when Nikki and Liam entered from the dance. Nikki was smiling from ear to ear, shocked to see me standing there in my suit.

I said, "May I have the last dance." We dance right there all dressed up in our finest in the kitchen. After the song, Nikki took Liam into bed. I lit a few candles around the house, changed the music to play softly in the background, and we held each other and danced a few more songs before we ended the night. It was one of the many memories I will treasure forever. Just a simple gesture to let her know just how much I loved her.

With summer soon approaching, I told Nikki it was time for her to have some much-needed alone time. Liam and I needed some much-needed father and son time, so I booked a trip for him and me to go to Universal for a few days.

Liam and I both really enjoy roller coasters. He was just barely tall enough to ride every ride. We started the first day off with the Hulk ride. Liam enjoyed it so much we did it three times in a row! Then, we walked to the Dr. Seuss section for him to enjoy while I recovered for just a moment. I don't think giggles stopped for either one of us for the entire day.

We spent one whole day at each park. We played I spy and charades while waiting in line for each roller coaster. We ate junk food and spent money on the silliest things. On the second day, it was a downpour for just a short period of time.

Liam started to look sad thinking our day was over. I got some ponchos, and we went puddle jumping in the rain. As fun as the rides were, this was the highlight to the day for me. Watching Liam's eyes light up as he jumped from puddle-to-puddle giggling. Jumping as high as he could to splash me as much as he could. Once the sun came back out, we finished up the day riding the rides We stayed one more night before driving back home.

Puddle Jumping at Universal

Once we got home, Liam went straight to Nikki and told her all about the trip. It warmed my heart to hear the first thing he told her was about the puddle jumping followed by the Hulk ride. These are the moments I have been dreaming of creating with them. I am so grateful I could have the opportunity to make them come true.

Father Son Day at Universal

The summer was filled with trips to the local water park, $5 movie days, Drive-Thru Palooza, backyard camping, and s'mores. Nikki joined in when she could, but this first summer was mostly about Liam and me. On the rare days off for Nikki, we would go to the beach or take a short-day trip somewhere. Traveling was something Nikki and I both enjoyed doing so we'd go somewhere new every chance we got. The summer ended, and back to the school routine we went.

CHRISTMAS

Time passed by so quickly being home. Before we knew it, it was Christmas. Christmas was simple for us, but for this year Nikki decided to drive to Indiana to pick up her grandmother to join us. Gam Gam always loved coming to visit. While I was away, Nikki would go to Indiana to pick up her sister, her kids, and Gam Gam, and bring them down for the summers. It was nice to be home for her whole visit this time.

Christmas gifts were kept to a minimum. Four gifts for Liam. Something you read, something you need, something you want, and something you wear. We actual adopted this for her nieces as well. For each other, we'd try to do something thoughtful and homemade if possible. Plus, we always had one gag gift for each other.

Christmas morning came. Liam, Gam Gam, Nikki, and I took turns opening our gifts. Smiles and laughter came with every present opened. Liam always asked to toilet paper as his need item to help the family out. It is always so fun to see the joy he gets out of opening a pack of TP every year.

This year I gave Nikki a Waffle House princess shirt because she loathes the place for some reason. Nikki got me the Ralphie bunny suit from my favorite Christmas movie, The Christmas Story. Liam's big gift this year was his first BB gun. He was so excited to go out and shoot.

As we cleaned up the wrapping paper, Nikki looked at me and said, "What's behind the TV?"

Liam ran over to the TV and said, "Papa, there is another present."

I retrieved the gift and sat to open it. To my surprise, Nikki had gotten me an AR. I had been wanting one for a while. I was so excited. I had my bunny suit and now I had the adult gun to go with it.

I looked at her and all I could do was say, "Wow, I can't believe you Ralphied me. Thank you, you're amazing."

Christmas Morning

Liam was excited for both of us to go shooting. Unfortunately, only he could shoot today. We set up his targets and learned some gun safety. Then, we enjoyed the rest of the day on the patio shooting and playing cards with Gam Gam. Once evening fell, we sat around the TV with fireplace playing on the TV and ate our Chili dinner. It's our family tradition to eat chili and sit by a fire for Christmas dinner. Though our new house doesn't have the fireplace anymore, the TV was good enough.

After dinner, we went for a drive to look at Christmas lights. It was such a fun-filled day. It was off to bed for us all because Nikki had a long drive ahead of her taking Gam Gam home in the morning.

Nikki and I made the most of every second we had off together. It didn't matter if we were getting a task done together, working in the shops, traveling, hanging out with friends, or spending time at home as a family.

We stayed extremely busy. Liam was growing like a weed. He was so smart and handsome. The years kept flying by with many amazing adventures along the way.

The job in Savannah was just the job for me. It had great hours, great benefits, and allowed me to be home nightly. It wasn't the most fun job I'd ever had, but it's worth it to be home. Being the guy who must tell people when they are messing up or must redo the job doesn't make you the most popular man in the hanger. It comes with the job, though.

I am Rob at work, but I go by Anthony to those who know me on a personal level. It helps me to leave work at work and home at home. I know it seems weird to some, but it helps keep me focused.

Fast Forward

Fast forward three amazing years and it takes us to 2019. This year started out amazingly. Nikki had a trade show in New York coming up in March. New York had been on our bucket list for a while now. Nikki went ahead of us to attend her trade show, then Liam and I flew in her last day and joined her. We enjoy so many things while there. Learning the subway, however, wasn't one of the things we enjoyed. We went to all the major tour sites, though. It was definitely an amazing place to visit, but it was now checked off. The only thing we missed was a Broadway show.

It turned out to be a huge year for the Cutting Cave team as well. We were so blessed to have grown the business so much, we were busting at the seams. We had fifteen stylists and two receptionists working for us. Our chairs were always full. The community had been amazing to us. Most days it was standing room only in the waiting room. It was time to look for a bigger place or a second space.

Touring NYC

Later in the year, one of the workers told Nikki about a local salon up for sale. Nikki went to see the location and knew it would be a great fit for us. It was close to Cutting Cave so the ladies who choose to work at the new location would be able to have their clients follow easier. We made an offer and just a few short weeks later we had a new location. Though we were excited, it would be a whole new level of stress for us both. There was lots to change to make it into what we needed, but it was a labor of love and worth it.

During the biding process, Cutting Cave also won their First National award from Salon Today Top 200 as the fastest growing salon in the nation.

Mind blowing! We were nationally recognized. We flew to New Orleans to accept the award. It was such an overwhelming experience. We took classes from the top winners. I learned a lot about the industry. The trip was well deserved for all the hard work Nikki, the team, and I put in. For me, it was a much needed few days with my beautiful wife, alone.

The first night there, we walked around sightseeing and then sat on a park bench to people watch. We talked about the unbelievable places and achievements we had made together. We dared to dream even more and even bigger. Nikki always joked how one day she would be my sugar momma, and how it might be sooner than we expected. We laughed as we got up to finish the walk back to the hotel.

Once we returned from our trip to New Orleans, we had a staff meeting to give everyone name tags and ribbons showing off their achievements. We made the announcement about the second location at this meeting as well. Everyone was excited and thrilled to be able to spread out and have their own space again. So, it was back to the grind for us to get this new location ready. It took us into the new year to complete the new location.

October 2019, we also celebrated our tenth wedding anniversary. To celebrate our amazing day, we decided to reenact our wedding photos! It was such a wonderful way to remember our beautiful day and to see how much we have changed. Our friend who has done nearly every family photo we have agreed to help us make this happen. The pictures turned out so much better than we ever expected, and we had so much fun making them happen. (You have to have to check these out on YouTube)

Celebrating Tenth Anniversary

COVID-19

During our renovations, COVID-19 hit the nation. Every industry was hit hard during this time, but salons/barbershops were hit extremely hard. We used the down time to revamp the old shop and complete the new one. It was how we paid our staff to still work even though we slowed down to a crawl.

Once we completed the renovations on both locations, it was time to open the new location. We set the date for April 1, 2020, to open Sheared Treasures. We changed the name of the new location to fit the needs of a family a salon environment. We wanted to create an atmosphere for families to enjoy.

Turned out instead of a grand opening we had a grand closing. The government shut down all barbershops and salons. We used this time to train our new staff at our new location and created fun stay-at-homework for our old staff.

I hated our businesses were closed, but we enjoyed our time at home together since it had been a while since we were all off at the same time. Nikki would work on the computer for half the day, then we would play games, go for walks, cook together, or do a cheesy craft she found on Pinterest.

Family Time During COVID-19

Being a business owner during these times hit Nikki hard mentally. Fear of losing everything, dealing with staff fears, and all the uncertainty was torture for her spiritually, mentally, and emotionally. Trying to navigate through these rough waters caused her to want to give up many times during the process.

Little did we know just how hard we would get hit by this virus. We went from being on top of the world to sinking sand. Our staff numbers kept dropping dramatically and quickly. We ended up with three at the new location and eight at the old.

Thankfully, we lived in Georgia and the governor allowed salons and barbershops to open in the first rounds of reopening. This move saved our business. We couldn't afford for either location to stay closed any longer. As soon as we had the four-page list of safety protocols, we got to work quickly to implement them all.

It was rough reopening with all the fears from the community as well as our staff. Safety was a priority, but we had to move forward. We went full steam ahead with both shops full of appointments getting all the clients we had on waiting list completed. We were grateful we had the new shop now so we could ensure the stylist were able to spread out the safe way.

We got the kinks out of the way and continued with business as the "new normal." It was miserable at first, but soon both shops adapted. We continued to lose staff, but we were able to keep our heads above water. Nikki and I sat down to discuss the possibility of having to let one go. Not what we wanted at all, but I it wasn't looking good for either location. Nikki didn't want the option, but she was so mentally exhausted she was ready to just give in.

Instead of giving up, we decided to take a trip to clear our minds and get out of town for little while. We decided to go to Washington DC.

DC was another bucket list place for us both. The sights were amazing to see in person. The night tour of the monuments was another great tour to take, I recommend it. The museums were a little underwhelming as they were using this slow time to remodel. We walked and walked enjoying all we could. The trip was filled with so much fun for each of us. We were only there a few days, so it was hard to try to squeeze everything in. There was more we wanted to see, so maybe one day we will make it back to finish what we started.

The trip was just what we needed. We came back renewed and ready to tackle our "new" reality. The trip reminded us it doesn't matter what happens with the shops. As long as we have each other, we will survive. We can rebuild and start again. We have individually rebuilt our lives from the ground up many times. The difference now was we would do it together.

We were blessed to win the Top 200 Fastest Growing Award again for 2020. This came at a great time for us. It lifted our spirits and helped to keep us determined to push through the uncomfortable situation we found ourselves in. Leaning on each other, we just kept pushing forward.

"Your hardest times often lead to the greatest moments of your life.
Keep going. Tough situations build strong people in the end."
- Roy T. Bennett[16]

[16] Goodreads.com

Chapter 16

FOCUS ON THE FAMILY

AS I LOOK back on 2020, it has many blessings and many struggles. Spiritual warfare (Nikki will write about in another book), shutdowns, betrayal, and business uncertainty to name a few of the struggles.

The blessings I can count are each day we spent enjoying our family, a trip we always wanted to take, and working together to rename and open a second location. I am grateful I was able to be a big part of this business beginning.

Nikki and I are stronger today than ever. With the pressure to succeed off our shoulders, we were able focus on today. No expectations of each other, we could stand together, and do the best we could like we did to get through everything life had thrown at us over the years.

Even though the life we worked so hard to build seemed to be crumbling all around us, we just focused on our family. Focused on what we could make better and let the rest fall as it will. At the end of the day, businesses and jobs can be rebuild or found. Our family was what we needed to focus on to withstand the test of time.

So, 2021 was the year we decided to focus on our family as much as possible and do what was important to us. We started off the year enjoying local places again. We visited downtown Savannah to see the new district recently completed. It was great being a tourist again around our town like we did many years ago. We went to the mall and rode around the mall on the motorized small animals. Man was it a great time. We giggled and laughed as we bobbed and weaved through the crowded mall. It was such a great day of joy for us. We finished the day with some ice cream on our way home.

We went back to the school and work until Liam's spring break. We went to Busch Gardens, Sea World, and had a short visit with some friends in Florida. Although Busch Gardens was a letdown with most rides and activities still shut down, we rode some rides, and enjoyed the day together anyway. Sea World though never disappoints. We had a great time watching the whale show. Liam and I rode rides as Nikki sat and enjoyed the dolphins. It was another short trip, but it was worth it to get away and continue to focus on our family.

Our New Normal

We stayed diligent with sanitation and followed guidelines everywhere we went, and in our shops, as well as at my work. Everyone seemed to be adapting and places were slowly opening the best they could. People were starting to come out again and feared a little less.

Our schedules returned to busy work weeks. Our stylist numbers were still falling as we went down to five at one shop and three at the other shop. We did everything right with honor and integrity. It was a great feeling knowing we were the type of bosses who could lay their heads down at night knowing we were who we set out to be and do. We did the impossible and stood true to who we are despite the sticks and stones people threw at us.

In June, Nikki had another trade show in Las Vegas. She hoped it would give her the fire back for the industry, I hoped it would give us another memorable vacation together.

Nikki flew out ahead of us as usual. Underestimating the summer heat, she was taken by surprise. She tried to sightsee the first night she arrived, but the heat was too overwhelming, and she went back to the hotel. She never got used to the heat, but she was better prepared the next day. Armed with tons of water, she went to the show, learned a few new things, saw a few new products lines she wanted to try out, but nothing too exciting to announce.

Nikki walked a few blocks to check out the city after the show. She didn't make it too far, but she was excited to see some of the sights. However, she was unimpressed with the city itself. She told me to expect New York

City with more naked people and drugs. As she returned to the hotel for the night, she grabbed pamphlets for things to do around the area away from the strip.

The next morning Liam and I left for the airport to start our journey to join her in Vegas. She attended the last day at the show as we flew there. Liam and I landed safely in Atlanta and enjoyed some Mexican food as we waited for our next flight. Liam and I always had a great time together. We had the same brain so it's easy to identify with him. We enjoyed some laughter and took some silly pictures to show Nikki of our journey.

We boarded the next flight and were finally off to meet Nikki. Nikki enjoyed a few more classes before leaving the trade show. Our flight landed just as her trade show let out. We took an Uber to the hotel and somehow beat Nikki there. We went to the room and waited for her to arrive moments later.

We wasted no time settling into the room and freshening up to head out to have dinner and sightsee. We decided to go to Senior Frogs inside our hotel for dinner, then set off to explore the strip. It wasn't long before I saw what Nikki was talking about. It had beautiful sights to see, but if you looked too closely it was nothing but trash and people asking for money from every tourist.

We watched the fountains dance, went into Caesars Palace to look around, and checked out a few other hotels as well. It had been a long day of traveling for us and walking for Nikki, so we decided to call it an early night.

We planned a week full of fun activities each one of us wanted to do. We started the week by renting two Polaris Spiders three-wheeler street legal vehicles. After getting our crash course on how to operate the cars, we were off to Red Rock Canyon. We drove the Red Rock Canyon National conservation area. It was so beautiful. It was such an amazing journey on a curvy road, through the red canyons, to the overlooks under beautiful sunny skies. Each stop had its unique shades of coloring and red tints to them. The ridged canyons told stories from the settlers of long ago. We looked out over sand dunes, too.

Liam rode with me through the winding roads. We had the music up and just cruised along. Nikki enjoyed the sights and the awe of God's creation. As she slowed to take it all in, I passed her then Liam and I sped up to enjoy our need for speed. We met up at the next overlook at the top of the mountain. Of course, Liam poked fun at her for how long we had been waiting for her to get there. We parked and walked a short trail to give our butts a short break. The heat was overwhelming, so we couldn't walk too far.

We returned to our little catch me if you can friendly game. Liam always enjoyed it when we would race each other home, so we thought why not race here, too. Nikki hated to race, but participated just to see the joy Liam and I got out of it.

Spider Cars

Nikki started off on the one-way direction all the way through the reservation. The roads were just wide enough to pass a normal sized car. If you got behind a large vehicle, you could forget about passing. Nikki rode in the middle of the lane so we couldn't pass her. Then we leapfrogged for a few miles to get the giggles and joy from Liam. We finally took the lead and left Nikki in our dust. She decided to go back to enjoying the sights around her, videoing, and thanking God for this opportunity.

Once we finish the thirteen-mile scenic drive, we headed off to grab some lunch and decide what was next on our agenda. As we ate, Liam picked on Nikki for losing the race. We just laughed and talked about how awesome the experience had been. We decided to drive back to downtown Vegas to check out Container Park, the shopping/entertainment section of Vegas made from shipping containers. It wasn't busy so we were able to shop and enjoy some ice cream before we returned the rented Spiders.

The heat drained us, so the evening was spent inside of the hotel with swimming and pizza before heading to bed early for our adventure tomorrow.

We got up at 4:45 a.m. to catch a tour bus to go to Hoover Dam, Route 66, and the Grand Canyon. It was scheduled to be a fifteen-hour tour. The first pick was us at 5:30 a.m. We were grateful to be the first pickup since Nikki gets car sick. We were able to get the first-row seats. The next thirty minutes we stopped at the other hotels around the area to pick up the rest of the tourists traveling on this tour with us.

At 6 a.m., we set off for the Hoover Dam. The ride to the Dam was rather quiet as most of those in the van went back to sleep, while the other half tried to wake up and enjoy the scenery along the way. Liam was one who went back to sleep while Nikki and I took in the sights along the way.

Hoover Dam

Once arriving at Hoover Dam, we piled out of the van and listened to our guide for our instructions. This was to be a quick fifteen-minute stop for a photo opportunity only. Everyone in the van took turns at different lookout points helping to take photos of each other's family. I had always wanted to see the Dam and take a tour behind the scenes. I want to come back for the tour one day. Nikki and Liam enjoyed the sight, but fifteen minutes was plenty for them.

We piled back into the van and stopped at a nearby hotel to use the restroom, shop in the souvenir shop, and grab some snacks. It was another quick fifteen-minute stop. Everyone on the van was awake and starting to have a few small conversations as we loaded up to head to Route 66. It was about two hours away, so we all put on our headphones and enjoyed our music as we watched the scenes go by out of the window.

Once arriving at Route 66, we stopped at the first gas station for fuel and restrooms. The town was Seligman, Arizona. It was the town the movie "Cars" was modeled after, so of course there were old cars made to look like in the movie strategically placed all throughout the town. It was a very historic town. We stopped at a few stores throughout the town and purchased our keepsakes, took some photos, and loaded to take off to the Grand Canyon. Nikki and I have been waiting our whole lives to see the Grand Canyon.

As we drove up into the Canyon, our tour guide began to give us instructions. This tour was to last for three hours. We followed him to a gorgeous overlook of the South Rim. The group took pictures of each other's families again. We were just completely awe stuck by this sight. It was breathtaking. As the tour guide struggled to get the group together again, he took us all to a path.

He said, "Follow this path and we will meet at the lodge three hours from now."

We hadn't known we were walking. Nikki and I were excited, but Liam said, "Nope, I'm going to stay in the van. I will see you on the other side."

Of course, we didn't allow him to do so, and we headed off on our journey. The long wait to see the Canyon was worth it for sure. We were able to appreciate the beauty of the colors, history, story, and the beauty at each overlook point. Each seemed more breathtaking than the last. We took picture after picture. Gorgeous is an understatement.

The path had many stops along the way with many signs about the history, museums, fun facts, and types of rock samples. We stopped often to take in the sights and have some water. Liam enjoyed himself reading the facts and being able to recognize some stuff he'd learned at school. It was another amazing family journey and a great memory for us.

Hiking in Grand Canyon

We got about an hour and half through our hike when some storm clouds started to roll in. We didn't care at first, but as they got closer, we knew we would get stuck in the storm. We still made the most of the journey, but we sped up our steps a little. The signs told us we weren't too far from the train depot resting area. Our goal was to make it there before the bottom fell out of those clouds.

We saw the Train Depot in the distance as it started to rain. The rain was rather cold at this elevation. We stopped to get Liam a hot dog before we entered the depot for shelter and restrooms. No sooner had we made it to the depot when the storm hit. Thunder, lightning, and a torrential downpour pounded the area. Nikki loves storms, so we just sat on the porch of the depot watching the storm pass. Liam enjoyed his snacks and the rest the storm brought.

We had about another half a mile to go before the pick-up point. With how cold the rain was and how hard it was storming, there was no way we could continue. I called the driver to let him know we were at the depot waiting for the storm to pass. Turns out most of the other groups on our tour were near our location, so he told us to all stay there and he would come to us. We missed the last short leg of our journey, but this trip was worth it. We will come back one day and do more!

After everyone made it back to the van, we set off for our long journey back to Vegas. Nikki and Liam slept as I stared out the window, grateful for this experience to make such amazing memories. It was a long day, but well worth every moment.

Storm Coming in Grand Canyon

The next day, we started our day at Circus Circus riding all the amusement rides they had inside the hotel. Liam had a great time riding one ride after another. I would ride one and sit out the next. We played arcade games and a round of mini golf. We were a little competitive with each other, so we played air hockey over and over. We enjoyed everything they had to offer. It was a great time of laughing and playing games together.

Once we finished a great day at Circus Circus, we decided to grab a bite to eat from a restaurant we had seen on TV. We headed off to Fremont Street to have dinner and sightsee. Once we arrived at the "old strip," we went into a few shops to gather a few souvenirs.

One of the shops had a sign, "Fish Kisses." Liam loving fish as much as he does, we had to head over to see what it was. As we got closer, we realized it was a pedicure shop using fish to eat the dead skin off your feet. I had seen this in other countries I've traveled to, but Nikki and Liam had never heard of such a thing. Of course, they had to do it.

They sat at the stations. I decided not to partake so I could just watch them. Once it was their turn, they sanitized their feet and put them into the water. As soon as their feet hit the water, the fish went to work. Nikki and Liam turned into five-year-olds, instantly laughing and giggling. I just couldn't help but laugh and giggle with them watching their reactions. Nikki and Liam talked me into getting one, too. I hate my feet being messed with, but why not. It was the weirdest feeling I have ever felt. My feet are extremely ticklish. I fought the urge to laugh out loud. Nikki and I both filmed each other and Liam just giggling away. After the fish finished eating off the dead skin, the gentleman dried off our feet and added some lotion making our feet as smooth as silk.

We headed to dinner at the restaurant we had seen on TV to enjoy the experience and the dinner. Once we arrived, we were given a hospital gown to put on before we headed to our table. Once we were seated, the waitress dressed as a nurse came to take our order and tell us the rule of the restaurant was whatever we order must be finished or we get spanked in front of the whole restaurant.

Liam and Nikki shared a fry and ordered a signal burger in fear of not being able to finish their meals. I ordered the heathy helping of a triple bacon cheeseburger and fries. I was sure I could finish it. Once the meal came, we all took a photo. Nikki and Liam completed their meals quickly. I was able to finish it all, but I left just one bite because Liam wanted to see me spanked.

I told him I would do it if he would do it, too. He giggled and said no way. Then he reluctantly said okay. When the waitress returned, I told her I just couldn't take the last bite and wanted to see if Liam could get spanked as well for not helping me finish the meal. We both stood up and walked over to the rail to hold onto.

The waitress made the announcement and got everyone's attention. Liam was up first. She gave him two gentle whips and then let him have it on the last one. Liam teared up. I grabbed him and told him how proud I was of him for getting in there when he didn't have to. Then it was my turn. The waitress held nothing back! I got three real good spanks. I won't volunteer to not finish my plate ever again.

We returned our robes as we exited the restaurant. We needed to walk off the dinner and the butt pain. We went to a few more stores on the old strip before heading back to the hotel.

Once we returned to the hotel, we showered and got ready for our last event of this trip. Nikki and I had booked a show to enjoy as a date night before we headed home in the morning. Once the show began, we were blown away by the comedy and the acrobatics. It was such a great performance. It was the perfect way to end our perfect vacation.

After the show, we walked slowly back to the hotel just enjoying the sights and each other a little longer. We played one slot machine just to say we did on our way up to the room. Then, we crashed as we had a long day of travels back to reality in the morning.

When we got home, it was right back to our daily routine. Liam started football practice for the first time. I was so proud of him for trying something new at a new school.

I told him, "Even if you fail or turn out to be no good at it, at least you tried and you know it's not for you. The worst thing you can do is not ever try."

Liam was new to sports and got frustrated along the way, but he stuck with it. I enjoyed watching him practice and seeing him get better every practice.

**"For God so loved the world, that he gave his only Son,
that whoever believes in him should not perish
but have eternal life.
For God did not send his Son into the world to condemn
the world,but in order that the world
might be saved through him.
Whoever believes in in him is not condemned,
but whoever does not believe is condemned already,
because he has not believed in the nAme of the
only Son of God."
- English Standard Version (ESV)[17]**

[17] The Holy Bible, English Standard Version copyright© 2001 by Crossway Bibles, aa publishing ministry of Good News Publishers.

OUR FINAL CHAPTER:

FRIDAYS CAME TOO fast for me. It was time to punch the time clock again. The day started off normal. One of the mechanics on the crew I was working with told his team he wasn't feeling well. He tried to call in, but he was out of PTO time, so his lead told him to get to work. After he arrived, when they saw how sick he was, they sent him home to go to the doctor. A few hours later, we were notified he had COVID-19 and the ones who worked with him that day were to quarantine for seven days.

I called Nikki immediately to let her know I had come in contact with someone with COVID-19, and I was headed home to quarantine. Starting that night, we stayed separated so if I did happen to get it, she and Liam wouldn't be exposed.

The first few days were miserable because I wasn't sick, but we stayed apart just in case. Those seven days didn't go by fast enough for me. Being home and not being able to be with my family was miserable.

We have a door in our bedroom to our backyard, so I often went out to get some sunshine. Just to be able to be with the family, I would text them to come outside. We would stay on opposite ends of the porch and just sit to talk. Liam enjoyed cutting down tree limbs, so one afternoon I sat and hung out with him from a distance while he cut down tree limbs in the backyard.

I also took this opportunity to let him do some more driving lessons in the backyard while Nikki was at work. Liam wasn't new to driving in the backyard, so he grabbed the keys and started the jeep right up. He drove it slowly to the big hole we had dug in our backyard. From a safe distance I gave him instructions on how to go into the hole and come out of the other side. He had so much fun going down into the hole. He enjoyed driving and I enjoyed being able to teach him new things. Even though I hated not being close to him, at least I got to be with him doing stuff.

The next time Nikki had a day off, we decided to go for a family drive. I would go out the back door and take the jeep while they would go out the front door and take the van. Not exactly together but together. We headed off to the local drive through wildlife preserve only to find out they had permanently closed. So, we headed to downtown Savannah to drive down River Street. I always forgot how bumpy it was.

We stopped for gas, then headed over to Wendy's for a frosty. Nikki went through and got me a frosty then put it on the front hood so I could retrieve it after she walked away. We sat in parking lot enjoying the ice cream and talking from a distance before we headed home.

Once home, I went back in the room. They sat down to watch a movie. I wanted to be with them, so I put a mask on and sat at the kitchen table to watch the movie with them. It wasn't ideal, but at least we were "together."

The next morning, I took the test again so I could hopefully return to work, but to my surprise I tested positive. Thank God I had stayed away from Nikki and Liam since being exposed. At least they wouldn't have to test or worry about being sick.

COVID-19 was like having a bad sinus infection, which I get often anyway. Once I knew I was exposed, we all had started taking the recommended vitamins. Once I tested positive, I reached out to my doctor for some medicine. There wasn't much he could do, but he tried steroids to help me get over the sinus infection feeling. The first few days weren't too bad. Taking the medicine and the vitamins had me hopeful I would be on my feet soon.

Nikki sanitized the doorknob then placed my meals right inside the door. All food was placed on paper plates and plastic cutlery so it could all be tossed out after I ate. Nikki went back to work mode the way she did while I was in Afghanistan so she could get everything done. I hated being home and not doing my part. As Nikki said my part was to get better. As hard as I tried to keep moving and not get worse, I seemed to be getting worse.

What started out feeling like a bad sinus infection started to become more like a bad flu. I called a doctor one of my co-workers used to get the "cure all pills" everyone was saying would cure the symptoms of Covid. It took just a few days to arrive, and I added them to the arsenal of medicine I was taking.

Two weeks after I tested positive, the flu-like symptoms had me down for the count. I ached, had chills, and so much coughing. I just couldn't seem to catch my breath once I start coughing. My chest started to feel extreme pressure and my breathing was getting more and more shallow and harder to do. I ordered an oxygen and heart sensor. Once they arrive, I started keeping up with my stats and my blood pressure.

As the oxygen levels started to drop, I would go to the hospital. They kept me overnight to get my stats back to 90, then sent me home to recover on my own. I begged them to let me stay so I could get better quicker. I was in extreme pain, and it was torture not being able to breathe. I didn't want to be away from Nikki and Liam any longer, I just wanted this over.

I went home and told Nikki what they said. It was only about me getting better. Every night, though, it was the same. My oxygen would drop to around 85/86, but would come back to 90 during the day. Sometimes it dropped quickly, but bounced back. I called the doctor, and he said as long as I kept going back up to 90, to stay home and wait it out.

One night, I dropped to 85/86 as I had been doing, but it just kept dropping from there. I ended up getting down to 82 and staying there for hours. I did everything I could think of to get it back up. Every breath was a struggle. I finally woke Nikki up at 5 a. m. and told her I needed an ambulance. I told her I had been at 82 for hours and to let them know I couldn't breathe.

I put on my mask and sat at the kitchen table waiting for them to arrive. Nikki woke up Liam and they both put on their masks to wait with me for the ambulance. I wanted so badly to grab them, kiss them, hug their necks, and feel them close to me one more time. However, I wouldn't wish this pain on anyone, so I kept my distance. I told them l loved them and walked to the ambulance.

Nikki just stood there crying and holding onto Liam assuring him I would be okay. It was the worst feeling leaving them, but I knew I needed to get some help. After a few hours in the ER, the doctor was going to do the same as the last hospital did. Get me to 90 and send me home. I texted Nikki to let her know which hospital I was in and I may be coming home again in a few hours, but I would let her know. After a few hours on the oxygen, I was able to get to 89.

The doctor came in and said, "Looks like the oxygen will get you to where you need to be soon, so I will get the discharge papers ready for you and..."

Suddenly, my oxygen fell to 79 right while she was standing there. I told her this was what kept happening. I'd get to 90 then I bottom out quickly.

The doctor said, "Well, I can't let you go home now."

I immediately called Nikki to tell her they were finally going to keep me, and I would get some much needed help.

Over the next few days, I stayed on 100 percent oxygen with the nose cannula. My chest X-ray showed I had Covid Pneumonia. I was relieved to be here getting help after all.

Nikki and I would FaceTime as often we could. The hospital refused visitors. Though she couldn't come up to me, she brought me some clothes, a puzzle book, my favorite snacks, and a picture of her and Liam she had given me for Christmas one year ago. I looked at the picture at least a million times.

Nikki and I treated this just like a ninety-day rotation we were used to from years back. I focused on the mission of healing, and she focused on getting the tasks at home tackled. I am grateful for technology allowing us to FaceTime and to have all my photos at my side. It seemed like all I could do was look at photos to keep me calm and get me through it.

It didn't take long, though, for loneliness to set in. Being this sick and not being able to have my loved ones near when I needed them the most was heart wrenching. I take pride in being mentally strong, but this was a whole new ballgame. Nikki kept assuring me I got this, but my mind was telling me otherwise.

My numbers would only improve for a short time. Any time I got up to use the restroom or tried to walk around the room, I dropped to the 70s again. The doctors decided to add more oxygen. They added a mask now with another 100 percent on it. I was also ordered to only get up to use the restroom until I was a little more stable.

I kept FaceTiming Nikki and Liam as often as I could, but talking through the mask was hard. I was just so frustrated I wasn't getting any better. I kept telling the doctors it felt like an elephant was sitting on my chest.

After I had been there for two weeks, I was still on two different types of oxygen at 100 percent each. When they did my chest X-ray, it showed my chest cavity had air in it. The pain was caused from taking a breath as it was putting extra pressure on my lungs.

The doctor called Nikki to update her on my condition. Once he told her air had seeped into my chest cavity and was putting pressure on my lungs, she asked him to go in and relieve the pressure.

The doctor stated, "We don't do it for these patients,"

She asked him to do so on her request.

He said, "It doesn't work on these patients so we won't need to do it, but his lungs do need a rest so I'm afraid we might have to put him on ventilator. We are trying not to go that route because it is last resort due to most people dying once ventilated."

Nikki agreed not to go that route. I didn't know about this conversation Nikki had with the doctor. I was having a conversation of my own with Jesus. He appeared in my room and stayed with me for two days. Nikki called while He was here, and I told her He was with me. She'd had encounters with Jesus before so I turned the phone camera around to the window where He was sitting to see if she could see Him.

She sadly said, "No, He isn't here for me, though, He is there to talk to you."

I told her we were working out our issues and taking things slow.

She assured me, "Take your time, Jesus will stay as long as He feels He needs to in order to help you work through your issues."

I hated to let Nikki go, but it was time I needed to talk with Jesus. Jesus and I talked for the whole two days. It was so amazing to be able to talk with Jesus about all my fears, frustration, anger, and the pack I had made with myself against Him when I was five. We talked about everything. He didn't dodge my questions. He didn't get upset at me for feeling the way I did. I must admit it was nice to not feel so lonely while He was with me. It was an unbelievable experience having Jesus take the time to be with me. He helped me, guided me, and taught me.

As we continued to talk, my heart softened and I completely broke. I explained to Jesus how I was a good man, but I had trouble getting rid of the hate in my heart towards those who tortured me for so many years. I struggled to let go of the hate because it helped me to guard myself over the years. Even though I worked daily on being a good man, the hate was what kept me vigilant, and I was able to read people for who they were.

Jesus just listened. He allowed me to break down and work out my feelings honestly for the first time. My demons had kept me bound for a long time. It was time to let Jesus into my heart and allow Him to heal me from the inside out.

Nikki told me not to rush into this and when I was ready to pray, use the simple prayer she texted me. After these two glorious days in our Savior's presence, I was ready. I pulled out my phone and read the text.

"Lord, I know I'm a sinner in need of Your grace. Please wash me clean and forgive me for my sins. I ask You to be Lord of my life. In Jesus name, Amen."

I was ready to let go of the hate and the past, and not allow it to be my driver anymore. It was like a huge weight was instantly lifted off me. I truly felt free. Shortly after I prayed, I drifted off to sleep. Once I woke up, Jesus was gone. I called Nikki to let her know I'd accepted Jesus into my heart. She immediately began to cry for joy and happiness for me. I began to cry for so many other reasons. I wanted her to know I knew if I died, she would see me again.

Once Nikki arrived at work, she sat in the car crying with me. It was so overwhelming. I told Nikki I didn't want to die with hate in my heart. As we both cried together on the phone, she begged me to stop. The fear of losing me was just too overwhelming for her. The fear of dying and leaving them was overwhelming for me. Crying was all we could both do.

Nikki had to go inside to work, and I needed to rest. Getting all worked up was bad for me. I just wanted sleep. Nikki couldn't pull herself together, though. She went inside to work and was immediately embraced by a co-worker. All she could do was cry. She knew things I didn't from the doctor's calls. She knew Jesus had been with me. She knew I was saved and had grace applied to my life. She was still trying to stay positive and hoped I would start improving.

I waited all day for her to get off work so we could pray together. I knew Nikki had been praying for this moment for thirteen years. I began to pray my first prayer with her, and when I got out of breath, I asked her to take over. What a blessing it was to be able to pray with her. I couldn't believe I had passed up this opportunity for so long. She was so happy we were praying together; she cried the whole way through our prayer and so did I. Ending the night with hearing each other's voices, hearing each other's prayers, and being able to say, "I love you" was what kept us going.

I got to the point if I tried to speak, my oxygen dropped, so I mainly just listened to Nikki and Liam tell me about their day. I was fighting with everything I had to get home to them. Liam was off to his first day of seventh grade and I got to see him in his new school uniform and hair looking all snazzy for his first day. I was beyond proud of him. He had become so handsome, too.

God, how did I get so lucky to have a son like him?

Nikki could see I was getting tired. She felt my spirits were dropping dangerously low. She reached out to everyone we knew me and asked them to send me Bible verses and up-lifting messages to try to lift my spirits. It was hard to keep fighting, but I knew what I was fighting for.

The next day, the doctor called Nikki and said I was headed in the direction of needing the ventilator. She again asked him to release the pressure around my lungs. He again refused. She told him she didn't want me on a ventilator and to keep trying. Within two hours, I called her with another doctor at my bedside.

This doctor told her they were taking me right then to be ventilated. She said no she didn't want it and she had already spoken to the other doctor. I told her I wanted it if it was my only hope and chance to coming home. I wanted to try anything to get home. As they wheeled me down the hall, I began taking all the oxygen off so I could talk to Nikki as clearly as I could.

I said, "I love you so much. Tell Liam I love him. I love you."

The nurse then took my phone and off I went. Nikki just fell to her knees and prayed for God to allow this to work and heal my lungs. She notified everyone I was being ventilated and to pray for better results than expected.

Nikki and Liam called every night. The nurse would prop the phone up next to my bed and allow them to talk to me. I couldn't speak, but I could hear them. I was fighting with everything I had, and I knew she was trying to let me know she was fighting for me in prayer.

This continued for seven days. I went up and down. Did better for a day and went backwards the next day. It was a lot of stress on my body and my family's emotions.

Nikki made her normal morning call on the seventh day. The nurses were not answering nor returning her call as normal. She felt something wasn't right. Turns out all the nurses and doctors where with me. My lungs just couldn't take the pressure anymore.

When the nurse finally called Nikki, they told her, "His lungs exploded."

They needed permission to do bedside chest tubes to relieve the pressure and re-inflate my lungs.

She let out a loud scream and said, "Of course, save him."

Her scream alarmed a co-worker. Nikki was shaking and crying fearing the worst. The ladies assisted her into the massage room to lay down and wait for the nurse to call back. As she waited, she called her best friend who is a nurse to ask her what it meant when they said my lungs exploded. Her friend immediately came to the shop to be with her knowing it wasn't good news.

As more of her friends were notified, she connected with the group chat for instant prayers for me. She didn't know it, but the prayers helped because I felt nothing as I slipped into Jesus' arms. The nurse called her again to let her know my heart had stopped and asked if they could try to restart my heart.

Nikki could feel everything happening to me. She was curled up on the massage table with everyone surrounding her screaming out. She was in agony. She knew the moment my heart stopped because I was standing in the room with her and her friends.

She heard me cry out, "I love you" one more time as I ascended into heaven. Once she shouted, "I love you" back she got the official call.

Though my heart did not restart here on earth, it now beats for an everlasting eternity in heaven. Nikki chose to never stop praying for my salvation and she never stopped believing in me.

I will await the day I get to meet Nikki and Liam at the pearly gates with open and loving arms to hold them for eternity. Until then, I will serve in the Lord's angel army protecting my family.

Hello friends,

My name is Nikki Scott. I wrote this book on behalf of my husband. Being his soul mate and being as one in Gods eyes, I felt our story needed to be told. I know our story, his story, can impact so many lives. It just needed to be told.

I was sure once he was saved, he would survive because the work for Christ we could have done together would have been so impactful. But like John Maxwell said, "be the legs to my legacy" which is what the Lord is calling me to do through the life of Anthony.

It was my absolute honor and privilege to be Anthony's wife and bear his only son Liam. He made me a better person and together WE created a life we could be proud of. WE chose daily to do better for each other. WE chose daily to seek a different life for ourselves. WE didn't settle for the lies Satan told us about who we were or where we came from. WE chose to listen to our inner spirit that God created in us. WE chose to listen to what God calls us to be.

We are His children.

We are redeemed because of Him.

He is our Father.

He is our provider.

He is our friend.

We are saved.

He is our healer.

He is the one to deliver us.

He is the great I AM.

He is whatever you need Him to be when you call on Him to be the one who meets your needs. I know I wouldn't be able to share our life experience and overcome them without God leading me. Without Him being the one who I call on when times get too difficult for me to bear. Because of my relationship with God, He has given me peace by letting me know Anthony is serving in His Angel Army. The question is... will we see you in heaven with us one day?

Thank you for reading about our journey and I pray you will seek God in all you go through.

Love, your sister in Christ,
Nikki Scott

Feel free to follow me on Facebook @ www.facebook.com/nikkimscott, on YouTube for some videos and picture slides to go along with what you have read Youtube.com/@Therighttimebook, or you can email me booksbynikkiscott@gmail.com

Picture made by: Chris Jeschkeit

ROBERT "ANTHONY" SCOTT WITH HIS ANGEL WINGS.

Journey Toward Hope:

CHAPTER 1: LIFE REFLECTIONS ON YOUR EARLY YEARS

As you continue to read about our story of how two extremely broken souls found love, comfort, passion, purpose, and fulfillment in each other through grace, love, and redemption, take a few moments to reflect on how your life started you on your journey.

What do you remember about the relationship between your mother and father?

____

____

Would you describe your family as dysfunctional or functional?
Explain:

____

____

How did the choices your parents made for each other and for you affect your life's journey?

____

____

What are your best early childhood memories?

____

____

What are your worst childhood memories?

____

____

Who did you turn to for help when traumatic events occurred in your childhood life?

____

____

I know revisiting past hurts and wounds can be overwhelmingly hard! Once you begin to remember it can change your mood, functionality, or keep you up at night. I urge you to press further through the pain. Pray throughout the process. Ask God to have the Holy Spirit wrap His arms around as you travel through the past.

We are not to camp out here, though! We are remembering so we can receive healing and can move forward.

When I was going through torture, it was hard to keep hope. I hoped daily today would be different. I hoped one day I would earn my family's love. I was just a young boy trying to figure out what I had done wrong to deserve the torture and rejection I received.

Finding the strength to keep going, will come from within you. God has already chosen you. His hope is within you.

Now, as I reflect on the early years with my parents, it breaks my heart they couldn't let go of their demons and past hurts.

I struggled for many years to let go of all the anger and resentment I had towards them, especially my father. When I realized I was only hurting myself to allow their actions towards me to affect my present life, I asked God to help me release them from my anger.

Use those experiences to help became a better father/mother. Asked for those generational curses to end with you. Allow your child to have the father/mother they deserve.

Your flesh will want to take the"easy" route. It's easier to stay bitter and angry because you know how to survive there. Forgiveness is the harder route, but I promise, once you forgive, you are truly free. You can heal and move forward. Learn from their mistakes. Use scripture to help you find the true peace only our God can give. Ask God to help you make peace with your past so you can live in the present!

Although my father and my mother have abandoned me,
Yet the Lord will take me up [adopt me as His child].
(Psalm 27:10 AMP)

Journey Toward Hope

CHAPTER 2: THE BOYS' FARM

LIFE REFLECTIONS

Torture, pain, and fear were what I knew and how I learned to survive. Even though more torture wasn't what I hoped for, knowing what it was like helped me to "survive" what was to come.

What defense mechanism did you use to survive the torture, pain, or fear you were subjected to growing up?

____

____

All the rage and anger had finally been unleashed. I had become a monster like my predators.

What became my breaking point that caused me to unleash the monster my predators turned me into?

____

____

How did I react when I became aware of what I had become?

____

____

How did I respond to God during this period of my life?

____

____

As I continued to pray for death or saving, a new spiritual battle started within me. After so much torture and hate from virtually everyone around me, I truly grew dark inside, and became numb to what was happening. I found myself trying not to become the monster I was being trained to become. However, the hate, bitterness, and anger just began to take over.

One evening as I returned to my room from another let's "chat in my room" meetings with a dorm parent, I prayed for God to save me or let me be killed. I was still too young to fight back, yet old enough to know there must be something better out there. After yet another night of praying fervently, but seeing no difference in my life, I vowed to God I would never ask Him for anything else as long as I lived.

Did you become angry even with God as you continued to see your prayers not answered the way you thought you wanted them to?

____

____

Describe what you were feeling:

____

____

This five-year-old-boy had seen unthinkable situations and been through unspeakable pain had finally had enough. I truly died that day and allowed my inner demons to protect me from then on. These kids and teachers would come to know me as a heartless, cold, soulless, bitter, and an angry child. For years, I watched many of my classmates go to insane asylums, kill themselves, or go back to their homes only to ruin their lives. As the cycle continued, I grew up believing that was my destiny and I accepted it.

How did what you believed about yourself affect your decisions as you grew older, stronger, and angrier?

____

____

From ages five to thirteen, I grew bigger, angrier, and darker. I was going to become so big and so mean, NO ONE would dare to mess with me again. Hate grew stronger, and bitterness ruled my every move. I just knew one day I could snap. Everyone would soon know not to mess with me again.

The Day I Snapped

One of the older boys come to "mess" with us younger kids, again. I was close to thirteen years old when I declared I was done taking it! I took every ounce of hate and anger inside of me and decided to fight back. I had never fought back before. I didn't know how to fight. What I could do well, though was take a beating. I "blacked out" as I always did to "protect" myself. I decided I would let him tire himself out taking punch after punch. However, this time I kept getting back up, refusing to allow him to beat me again. He became exhausted within minutes. His punches were slowing, and he was starting to breath harder.

Does this reflect what you were thinking and experiencing?

____

____

This was it. I saw my chance. I hit him with everything I had knocking him to the ground. I then got on top of him and started choking him. Still in the "black out" state, I held him until I felt his body go limp and he took his very last breathe.

All the rage and anger had finally been unleashed. When I "snapped out of it," I looked up into the crowd that had formed around us. I saw everyone staring at me in fear. It was the way I had looked at my "predators" all these years.

I thought this was what I wanted. However, I discovered I didn't want to see myself become this monster. This wasn't who I wanted to become.

Ask yourself, do I really want to become like my predators or is my goal to become something better?

____

____

History has often shown that the abused become abusers. Why does this happen?

____

____

He heals the brokenhearted and binds up their wounds
[healing their pain and comforting their sorrow].
(Psalm 147:3 AMP)

"Dissociation is an emotional protection strategy that totally
and completely removes painful realities from the mind
and body of the survivor."
- Kathy Broady[18]

There are many scars from experiencing abuse, especially childhood abuse. One of the defenses even young children can develop to deal with the

[18] Goodreads.com

trauma of abuse is dissociation. This occurs when the trauma is so intense our normal ability can't cope with it.

Though dissociation may help the child deal with the abuse or neglect, the trauma that caused the dissociation may need to be dealt with when the child reaches adulthood. This is when a loving spouse or a trained Christian counselor can help one to be able resolve the issues caused by the trauma.

Journey Toward Hope

CHAPTER 3: MEANWHILE, IN INDIANA...

NIKKI'S STORY

LIFE REFLECTIONS

Nikki realized she had been lucky to survive alcohol poisoning. This was the last straw. She wanted a different life. So, she went back home and begged her mother to let her stay there saying all she wanted was to be with her family again. Her mother agreed if she would agree to stop her drugs and drinking.

At what point in your journey did you decide you no longer wanted to live a destructive lifestyle?

____

____

Though many of her peers thought Nikki was living the "teenage dream life," after over a year on the streets and having things "happen" that happen to drunken underage girls willing or not, she was ready to return home and try to be the daughter her mother wanted her to be.

Did you think you wanted a life of freedom only to discover what that freedom was costing you?
Explain:

____

____

Nikki, her mom, and sister didn't know how to be a family, but she knew she didn't want to be alone anymore.

NIKKI STAYED STRONG THROUGH ALL THE CHANGES BECAUSE SHE STILL WANTED TO DO BETTER FOR HERSELF.

What kind of example did you have of a productive, love-filled family?

____

____

What advice would you give to teenagers to avoid the pain and trauma you experienced?

____

____

> *The Lord is close to the brokenhearted and saves those who are crushed in spirit.* (Psalm 34:18 NASB)

Many teenagers seek the freedom to do whatever they want with no rules and no boundaries. They think this would be the ideal life and may make choices that bring destructive consequences they had not anticipated. Nikki discovered this level of "freedom" did not really bring freedom at all.

She ended up in "bondage" to drug and alcohol addictions that nearly cost her life. She also dealt with shame, guilt, and a loss of purpose for her life after living the freedom of a street life for a year.

SHE DISCOVERED ALL SHE EVER REALLY WANTED WAS FOR SOMEONE TO LOVE HER AND TELL HER SHE DIDN'T NEED TO LIVE THIS WAY.
SHE LONGED FOR SOMEONE TO TELL HER SHE HAD A PURPOSE IN LIFE AND SHE WAS MEANT FOR MORE THAN WHAT HER BODY COULD BE USED FOR.

Don't trade one kind of bondage for another. Seek true freedom through a relationship with God through Jesus who willingly gave His life so you could be set free from the bondage of sin.

Will you turn your heart toward Him today, confess your sins, ask for His forgiveness, and allow Him to cleanse you white as snow?

Journey Toward Hope

Chapter 4: Back in Texas

Robert's Story

Life Reflections

There were three decisions I made that would eventually change my life's direction.

1. I decided I would return and face my punishment.

   How much courage did it take for Robert to decide to go back and face the consequences of his actions?

   ____

   ____

   Have you had to make a similar decision?
   Explain:

   ____

   ____

2. I declared I wouldn't let them win.

   Have you had to deal with a bully?

   ____

   How did you handle the situation?

   ____

   ____

3. I determined I wouldn't allow myself to become one of them!

   Use positive self-talk to overcome what others say you are or are not.

   ____

   ____

When all you know is heartache and pain,
heartache and pain are all you seek.
It's comfortable, it's familiar.
The unknown and love become scary.

Ask yourself, where should I go to search for who I want to be?

This search begins with prayer. Pray and ask God to reveal how He sees you.

Who does God say you are in:

Romans 8:17
Psalm 139:13-14
2 Timothy 1:9
Colossians 2:10
1 Thessalonians 1:4
2 Corinthians 5:17
1 John 3:1

Journey Toward Hope

CHAPTER 5: NIKKI'S SCARIEST MOMENT

LIFE REFLECTIONS

Nikki made a dangerous choice that changed the course of her life for many years. She thought she was doing what was right.

What did you learn from reading how this choice changed Nikki's life?

____

____

The choice she made had a snowball effect that led to many more poor choices.

How has Nikki's story made you more aware of how important making right choices are to in your life?

____

____

Journey Toward Hope

Chapter 6: Robert and Nikki Continue Their Separate Journeys

Notice how both Robert and Nikki were seeking to find out who they were and how to keep hope alive on their life's journey.

Describe a time when you were in a similar place on your journey: search for who I want to be?

Notice how God was subtlety moving each of them individually in the right direction to bring them together to fulfill His plans and His purpose in each of their lives.

Looking back at your journey, where do you see God's hand on your life to bring you to where He could fulfill His divine purpose in your life?

____

____

"The best way to find yourself
is to lose yourself in the service of others."
- Mahatma Gandhi

Nikki found this quote from Mahatma Gandhi to be true.

How did deciding to help others help her to deal with the pain and suffering she was dealing with in her own life?

____

____

Have you found this to be true in your life's journey?
Explain:

____

____

How can you help others come to this realization in their lives as well?
Nikki discovered the only way to truly fill that void in her life was what?
Have you been trying to fill the void in your heart in all the wrong ways?
______________________ *If yes, what do you now need to do?*

____

____

One of the exercises from the "Making Peace with your Past" book by H. Norman Wrigth.

To help you release yourself from the past, the first step is to write a letter to each person you need to release from your past. Be honest with yourself! Let it all out! Don't hold back one thought or emotion you have been holding in for years. Now is your chance. It will be emotionally draining. I won't lie, it is tough, at times excruciating but pray through it. Welcome God into your space. Get cozy, now let it out on paper. Be sure to end the letter with a true from the heart, "I forgive you."

The second step is to sit with two chairs facing each other. Picture the other person sitting across from you. Now read your paper out loud to them. Read each letter to each person. Allow yourself to express everything to them. Allow yourself to release every person. Between letters, allow yourself to feel the release from the anger and sadness of betrayal. Allow yourself to be free from each person on by one. *(Side note Nikki pretended to write her letters to Jesus instead of the people.)*

The third step is to burn each letter AFTER you read out loud. Make a cozy fire. Sit and throw each letter one by one into the fire and watch until they each are completely burned into ashes. Sit for a while and enjoy your newfound peace. Feel God's presence in this moment. Allow yourself time to take a deep breath. Allow yourself to start to replace each emotion with positive praise.

Don't forget the most important part is prayer over your time doing this. Ask God into this process. Ask for His protection and for His peace to wash over you. Ask Him for forgiveness as you have now forgiven those who trespassed against you. Praise Him for adopting you as His child.

We always advise you to seek professional advice or counseling before doing this activity.

Chapter 7: The Beginning of Us

Anthony and Nikki's paths finally cross just a few weeks before Nikki plans to move back to Indiana.

Describe a time when you thought you had figured out the next move on your life's journey, but something happened to make you consider changing those plans.

Life Reflections

Notice how God's timing came just on time to keep them moving in the right direction.

Has this happened to you?
Explain:

____

____

____

Did you think it was just causing chaos at the time?
Describe how you handled it:

____

____

Journey Toward Hope

CHAPTER 8: THE PREGNANCY

Have you ever had a word of prophecy spoken over you and wondered if it would truly happen?
Explain:

____

____

What emotions did you experience (joy, fear, hope, anticipation…)?
Did the prophecy come true?

LIFE REFLECTIONS

Have you experienced a time when a fear something bad was going to happen?
Explain:

____

____

How did you handle this fear?

____

____

Did the way you reacted and handled your fear help or hinder you?

____

____

Journey Toward Hope

Chapter 9: Getting Ready for Liam's Arrival

Anticipating the arrival of a baby creates all kinds of emotions in the parents.

How was your preparation time as you waited for your child's arrival?

____

____

What changes did you anticipate happening after your child arrived?

____

____

Life Reflections

Finally, at 34 years old, I could say, I have known love and I can love completely.

Have you had the beautiful experience of finding a loving spouse and receiving a beautiful child to fill your life with joy and love?
Explain:

____

____

Was the journey easy all the time?
Explain:

WE KNEW LIFE WOULD GET BETTER.

We knew life would get better. It just takes work and a lot of it.

What life experience has made you fully believe this truism?

Journey Toward Hope

CHAPTER 10: LIFE'S CHALLENGES

Being married was amazing! However, our marital bliss was soon challenged when I found out I was losing my job. Sometimes life sends us challenging circumstances like losing your job.

Communication is always the key to working through marriage problem solving.

What unexpected challenges have you had to face?

____

____

What have you learned about communication?

____

____

How did you decide to proceed with your life journey?

____

____

Life Reflections

We had to build the ladder of our relationship piece-by-piece, step-by-step. We didn't have anyone to give us an example of how to do this.

Did you have a good example to show you how to build a lasting marital relationship?
Explain:

____

____

How did observing failing relationships show you what not to do?

____

____

Journey Toward Hope

CHAPTER 11: THINGS START COMING TOGETHER

The jewelry lady said, "I don't know you, but you need me. It's written all over your face you are mommy all the time and it shows. Meet me tomorrow at 11 a.m. for coffee."

Nikki agreed because she knew she needed something. Nikki wanted and needed what this lady had discovered.

What had the jewelry lady discovered Nikki needed?

____

____

What did you discover from this Chapter you need?

____

____

What do you need to do to get what you need for your life's journey to continue productively?

____

____

Life Reflections

I can say finding my soulmate in Nikki and being a father to Liam have given me purpose. I have found my place and my "why" in this life in my family's arms.

Have you gotten to the place where you know your family and their love is worth fighting for?

____

____

Have you found your purpose in their loving arms? ________

If not, what do you need to do to make this a reality in your life?

____

____

Declare:

- *My family deserves to receive the best version of me.*
- *I choose to fight through my thoughts to be a better person each day.*
- *I desire to give my best to my family in all I do.*
- *I want to be the person deserving of their love.*
- *I want to be proud of the person I am to those around me.*
- *I seek to display integrity, honor, respect, and loyalty in my life today and every day.*

Journey Toward Hope

CHAPTER 12: OUR LIVES CHANGE AGAIN

One of my coworkers told me,
"If you do for two years what others would never do,
then you would be in a place they would never be."

I took his words to heart. I was willing to put in the work to get my family to a better place. It took sacrifice and dedication, but it was worth it because my family was worth it.

What vision do you have for your family you know is going to take hard work, sacrifice, and dedication to achieve?

____

____

DECLARE OUT LOUD: MY FAMILY IS WORTH IT!

LIFE REFLECTIONS

THE CUTTING CAVE

Nikki would be able to give women a safe place to work. A place to grow their skills, faith, and finances. We would be able to provide a working environment we could be proud of. Even if we failed, we were brave enough to try.

Are you and your spouse brave enough to take a step of faith and move toward fulfilling your vision to help your family and others?

What is the first step you need to take to get started on this new journey?

____

____

Journey Toward Hope

CHAPTER 13: LOVE, LIFE, AND LOSS

Often, we can get so busy with our everyday routines, we forget to be grateful for the love of our spouse and children. We may even begin to take them for granted. Don't allow that to happen in your life.

Make a list of ways you can show appreciation to your spouse for their love, support, and faithfulness.

Life Reflections

This tragedy reminded us just how precious life is, and how quickly it can be over.

> *Have you taken the time to count your blessings for love and life? List your blessings and thank God for each one.*

____

____

____

____

____

____

Journey Toward Hope

CHAPTER 14: HOME FOR GOOD!

There are times in our life's journey we must make choices which keep us away from our families for a time. No matter how mature and strong our family relationship is separation can put a stress and strain on our family unit.

Has your family experienced a time of necessary separation?
How did each family member handle it?

____

____

____

____

How would you advise other families ways to effectively handle separations?

____

____

____

____

Life Reflections

"Families are the compass that guides us.
They are the inspiration to reach great heights,
and our comfort when we occasionally falter."
- Brad Henry[19]

Though Nikki and I did not experience this in our growing up years, we were determined to make this true for our family.

If you did not have a positive growing up experience in your family, how have you worked to set a good example for your children and other families around you?

____

____

____

____

[19] Goodreads.com

Journey Toward Hope

CHAPTER 15: LIVING OUR BEST LIFE TOGETHER AGAIN

We found being home and sharing the family load together is what life is about.

How has your family worked together as a team to share the workload especially if both parents work full time?

____

____

LIFE REFLECTIONS

We all remember the fears and changes associated the COVID-19 virus pandemic.

How did you and your family handle all the changes and fears COVID-19 brought to your community?

____

____

Journey Toward Hope

Chapter 16: Focus on the Family

I told him, "Even if you fail or turn out to be no good at it, at least you tried and you know it's not for you. The worst thing you can do is not ever try."

It was a great feeling knowing we were the type of bosses who could lay their heads down at night knowing we were who we set out to be and do. We did the impossible, stood true to who we are despite the sticks and stone people threw at us.

Have you stood true to who you know you are supposed to be in spite of what the world around you says you should do or be? ________

If not, what changes do you need to make in your life?

____

____

Life Reflections

Even though the life we worked so hard to build seemed to be crumbling all around us, we just focused on our family. Focused on what we could make better and let the rest fall as it will.

How has this Chapter helped you to seek to focus on your family even in the tough times?

Journey Toward Hope

LIFE REFLECTIONS

As you read our final Chapter together on earth, I hope it encouraged you to seek the Lord for your own salvation, As you read, death can come unexpectedly. You need to choose where you want to spend eternity.

Read these verses concerning God's gift of a life with Him through eternity.

John 3:16-18 tells you why God is offering you this free gift.

Ephesians 2:8-9 confirms this offer of salvation from God is a free gift and not earned by works.

Romans 6:23 again verifies why you need salvation, and it is a free gift from God through His Son Jesus.

Acts 13:47 explains there is salvation in no one else.

1 John 1:9 tells you how to gain the Lord's forgiveness and receive salvation.

In John 14:6, Jesus tells you He is the only way to salvation.

In John 3:3-6, Jesus tells you the only way to eternal life with Him is to be born again.

John 1:12-13 gives you the benefits of receiving this free gift.

Titus 2:11-14 tells you salvation is for everyone.

1 Thessalonians5:9-10 says God does not want to punish us, but offer His salvation to us through Jesus's death and resurrection.

When you are ready, say this simple prayer and receive God's free gift of salvation through Jesus, His only Son.

God, I thank You for sending Your precious Son to die for me on the cross. I believe He rose again from the dead and has conquered death for me. I ask Him to forgive my sins and become my Lord and Savior. Thank You I am now Your child and can spend eternity with You through Christ my Lord and Savior.

CPSIA information can be obtained
at www.ICGtesting.com
Printed in the USA
JSHW010739210623
43510JS00002B/8